THE BRITISH RAJ NOVELS

THE BRITISH RAJ NOVELS

A COLONIAL HANGOVER

P. A. ATTAR

PARTRIDGE

To order additional copies of this book, contact
Partridge India
000 800 10062 62
orders.india@partridgepublishing.com

www.partridgepublishing.com/india

CONTENTS

Dedicated to

My *Alma Mater*

Shivaji University, Kolhapur

Acknowledgement

I wish to express my deep sense of gratitude to Hon. Vice-Chancellor, Professor Devanand Shinde, Professor Manikrao Salunkhe, Professor N. J. Pawar, Professor P. R. Kher, Professor S.K. Desai, Professor J. A. Shinde, Principal Dr. D R More, Professor V. V. Badve, Professor C J Jahagirdar, Professor Maya Pandit, Professor M. L. Jadhav, Mr C G Attar, Mr Sultan Attar, Dr Sharad Navare , Dr Uday Narkar and Dr. K. S. Chaugule for their valuable guidance and constructive criticism.

This study was made possible by the award of Teacher Fellowship by the University Grants Commission, New Delhi and the grant of study leave by Shivaji Education Society, Karad. In this respect I am particularly obliged to the Late Shri. Y.B. Chavan, former Deputy Prime Minister of India, Shri P. D. Patil, former Chairman, Shri Shivaji Education Society, Karad and P T Thorat, former Principal of Venutai Chavan College, Karad

I would also like to thank Dr. Francine Weinbaum, Illionois University (U.S.A.), and the Director, David Higham Associates, London, who provided me with the rare resource material on Paul Scott. Warm thanks are also due to my friends Professor Rambhau Badode, Dr. Ashok Thorat, Professor Hamid Khan, Professor Vijay Fulari, Dr. C. A. Langre, Dr Trupti, Dr Prabhanjan, Dr Akshyay, Dr Rajashri, Dr Vasvani, Dr. Sudhir, Dr. Yasmin, Aiman and Aijaj.

Among the institutions which helped me, I must make a grateful mention of the British Council, Bombay, American Studies Research Centre, Hyderabad; Central Institute of English and Foreign Languages, Hyderabad, University of Poona, Pune, University of Delhi, New Delhi, the National Library, Calcutta, and Shivaji University, Kolhapur.

If by some mischance I have failed to acknowledge where I should have done so, I hope those concerned will accept my apologies.

Kolhapur   P A Attar

PREFACE

Paul Scott (1920-1978), a modern Anglo-Indian novelist of great distinction, who is the winner of England's two coveted prizes, the Yorkshire Post Fiction Award in 1972 and the Booker Prize in1977, is perhaps the best known writer of the British colonial experience in India during its twilight days. Born in London in 1920, Scott served in the army from 1940 to 1946, mainly in India and Malaya. After getting back to England he worked for a publishing company for four years before joining a firm of literary agents. In 1960 he resigned his directorship with the agency in order to concentrate on his own writing. In 1963 he was elected a Fellow of the Royal Society of Literature. He wrote thirteen distinguished novels including much acclaimed *Raj Quartet* and also reviewed books for *The Times, The Guardian, The Daily Telegraph and The Country Life*. The fact that several of his novels have been adopted for radio and television accounts for the recognition of his works on a wider scale.

A brief resume of the major critical responses received by Scott proves the fact that he still needs a wider critical attention to have a deeper insight of his novels. At the moment his *Raj Quartet* is the only work that has received extensive critical attention. The generally accepted verdict that *The Raj Quartet* is Scott's greatest achievement is confirmed by the fact that it has aroused a considerable interest among critics since its publication. Its position of acknowledged greatness, therefore, certainly demands a reference to various critical responses to it. John Mellors, for instance, considers it important because, by evoking the final episode in the 'long and passionate affaire'[1] between British and India, it contains something of all the issues Scott wants to raise: justice, responsibility, political expediency, law and order, sex and race, pride and prejudice, love and loyalty.

John Leonard, an American critic, in his review article published in *the New York Times* on the occasion of Scott winning the Booker Award, considers the issue yet from altogether a different point of view and considers *The Raj Quartet* from a racial point of view. He, therefore, states:

> Andrew Young was right: the British did invent racism. And it
> is something more than a doctrine or a policy, something more

than an attitude. It is psychopathology, a form of cultural sadomasochism, with its own etiquette, dreams, demons, denials, myths, tormented exceptions, and built-in death wish. The proof is in Paul Scott's *The Raj Quartet*.

Leonard is very clear in his assessment of Scott in terms of racial relationship since the interaction between the British and the Indians was a very crucial problem then since the entire colonial affair was based on the myth of white superiority.

Francine Weinbaum, another American critic, thinks how Scott has presented a picture, politically, sociologically, and psychologically revealing, how the two nations came into tragic confrontation, and how and why British rule ended in a sense of diminished stature. Patrick Swinden, perhaps the only critic who has given a comprehensive critical attention to all of Scott's novels, reckons Scott to be one of the best English novelists to have emerged since the war. In his opinion, the implications of what Scott writes about questions of national and racial identity, his speculations about the realities and illusions of the personal life and their relationship to public responsibilities, are not restricted to life in India or to the political complexion of those five years (i.e., 1942-1947). They are moral and metaphysical questions which are subtly and profoundly answered in these novels. Max Beloff, a modern British historian, stresses the point that the novelist's advantage over the historian is most clearly seen in *The Raj Quartet* because, according to him, only few historians have treated the fall of the British Empire as something that did not have to happen in the way it did.

No doubt, most of these critics have to contribute in their own ways to the understanding of Scott's novels. However, my assessment of the novelist makes a point of departure in the sense that it treats Scott as a historical novelist. Scott must be placed high on the list of the writers who have shown their vital concern with history, especially on the list of those who have been involved in writing on the theme of foreign occupation or dismantling of empires.- In the inter-war decades there appeared in the literature of colonialism the relatively new theme of decolonisation and since Paul Scott is the major British novelist writing on the decline and fall of the British colonial hold on India a study of his work in terms of the parameters of historical fiction becomes imperative. In the present book my attempt has been to make a full-length study of Scott as a historical novelist with special reference to his Indian historical novels. However, I believe that the theory of historical fiction, if it is to be useful must be recognised as being provisional and for convenience only.

In this prefatory note it remains only to be said that the seven novels that form the subject of the detailed analysis in this book are those in which, I feel, Scott shows his essential qualities as a historical novelist.

P. A. Attar

CHAPTER I

Introduction

I. Some Definitions of Anglo-Indian Literature
II. Historical Background of Anglo-Indian Literature
III. The Concept of Empire and the British Raj in India
IV. Brief Resume of Anglo-Indian Fiction

INTRODUCTION

I

Some Definitions of Anglo-Indian Literature:

India has fascinated Europe from time immemorial. The imperial idea which fired the imagination of the English for almost three centuries inspired a vast body of literature, especially fiction written in the context of the British Raj in India. "Anglo-Indian Literature", as this body of literature is called, has been described by a few scholars. Writing in 1908, for example, E.F. Oaten described it as follows:

> Anglo-Indian Literature, as regards the greater part of it, is the literature of a comparatively small body of Englishmen who, during the working part of their lives, become residents in a country so different in every respect from their own that they seldom take root in its soil. On the contrary they strive to remain English in thought and aspiration.... Anglo-Indian Literature, therefore, is for the most part, merely English Literature strongly marked by Indian local colour.[1]

Oaten seems to be somewhat vague in attempting the definition as he has not given the clear cut distinction between Indo-Anglian and Anglo-Indian Literature. For example, in the concluding part of his critique he considers Michael Madhu Sudan Datta and Govind Chand Datta as Anglo-Indian writers, who, in fact, can be treated as the Indo-Anglian writers or the Indian English writers. However, this ambiguity can be understood since the book was written in 1908 when the body of Anglo-Indian Literature was relatively small. Bhupal Singh, an Indian scholar, who also attempted the definition of Anglo-Indian Literature, appears ambiguous when he writes:

> Broadly speaking it (Anglo-Indian fiction) includes any novel dealing with India which is written in English. Strictly speaking it means fiction mainly describing the life of Englishmen in India. In a still narrower sense it may be taken to mean novels

dealing with the life of Eurasians who now prefer to be called Anglo-Indians.[2]

Oaten's ambiguity is still not removed by Bhupal Singh in the sense that, he too, like Oaten, does not discriminate between the Indo-Anglian and Anglo-Indian writers. For example, he regards Bankim Chandra Chatterjee, a nineteenth century writer, who, in his romances, mainly dealt with the secret societies of young men dedicated to the service of the Motherland, and Panchapakesa Ayyar, an Indian Civil Servant and a historical romancer, as Anglo-Indian writers.

One more considerable attempt made by John A. and Leena Karkala, who call Anglo-Indian Literature as the nebulous body of literature, pay special attention to the different meanings of the term 'Anglo-Indian' - one taken in India and another in England and elsewhere. In India, according to them, 'Anglo-Indian' means a person of Eurasian origin.' The Anglo-Indian community in India has not produced a sizable body of literature which could properly be called 'Anglo-Indian Literature'. Perhaps the only exception is Henry Derozio, the nineteenth century boy-poet of Calcutta. In England, the term 'Anglo-Indian' has slightly different meaning, probably suggesting some kind of interaction between Anglo-Saxons and Indians. Consequently, Anglo-Indian Literature, from the British point of View, "has been literature produced by Englishmen while on active service in India, but essentially recounting their Indian experience". Anglo-Indian Literature also includes literature produced by British citizens born in India and for some part of their life brought up in that country, but who essentially remained British in their way of life and attitudes.[3] This distinction demands special attention because it, for the first time, takes the writer's origin or nationality into account which distinguishes him from the Indo-Anglian writer who is regarded of Indian origin. K.R.S. Iyengar considers it yet from another point of view and holds that

> "unfortunately, the word 'Anglo-Indian' has also a racial connotation; Eurasian, Anglo-Indian - these words are sometimes used with a snigger and evoke 'chee-chee' feeling; and the so-called Anglo-Indians themselves are not now anxious to retain this name, and are happily content to merge with the Indians or Pakistanis. And it was not the Anglo-Indians in this narrow sense that created the main body of Anglo-Indian Literature."[4]

Though Iyengar classifies the writers like Sir William Jones, Sir Edwin Arnold and Meadows Taylor as Anglo-Indian writers, he does not feel it necessary to consider this body of literature as an independent genre when he says that the work of a Kipling or a Forster belongs properly to English literature; just as Pearl Buck and Luis Broomfield, even when they choose to write about India, should be classed as American writers. There are some scholars, like H.M. Williams, who believe that the terms 'Anglo-Indian' and 'indo-Anglian' are tentative and clumsy, as well as ambiguous. But still the distinction is needed to avoid the confusion.[5] The term 'Anglo-Indian' as used by Allen J. Greenberger in *The British Image of India: A Study in the Literature of Imperialism, 1880-1950 (1969)* and Benita Parry in *Delusions and Discoveries; Studies on India in the British Imagination - 1880-1930* refers to the literature written by Englishmen in India'. The term "Anglo-Indian Literature" as I have used it, denotes a reflection of British consciousness in the context of British Imperial Rule in India.

II
HISTORICAL BACKGROUND OF ANGLO-INDIAN LITERATURE

The British Raj is one of the most important occurrences of history since it has exercised a considerable influence not only in the spheres of law and administration, but also in the realms of ideas and creative literature. The British first came to India as traders, with no intention of assuming political responsibility for any Indian territory. During the early seventeenth century, the English East India Company began to establish trading stations along the Indian coast. The Moghul power in India by this time was waning rapidly, and when Emperor Aurangjeb died in 1707, warring Indian princes began to vie with each other to grab the political power. Both the English and the French took advantage of this unstable situation to extend their influence. Gradually the English gained upper-hand over their French rivals and by the close of eighteenth century, after the military exploits of Robert Clive and the political and administrative consolidation of Warren Hastings, virtually the whole subcontinent was dominated by the English Company.

Gradually, therefore, the Company was transformed from a trading venture into an administrative organization, increasing its profits with the taxes it collected. The British Government gradually decided to intervene directly in Indian affairs, and finally took over control in 1858. Thereafter, although some parts of India were placed under direct rule, many of the interior princely states were ruled only indirectly, enjoying a certain amount of autonomy. British governors in each province were responsible to the Viceroy who was appointed by Parliament in London. In 187 Queen Victoria was declared Empress of India.

In 1885, the Indian National Congress was formed to agitate for a greater degree of native self-rule but at first it was little more than a debating society only. In 1906, the Muslim League was established to advance the cause of Islam in India. In the years immediately before and after World War I the struggle for national independence began to override communal and religious differences among Indian population. Although Indians were now elected to local legislative bodies, the British at first tried to counter this trend with repressive measures.

The War that broke out in 1914, however, brought about profound changes not only in Britain's position in the world but in Britain herself. These changes resulted in new attitudes towards her responsibility in, and to, India. After 1918, the British power, already weakened within, received new challenges-from the new fascist imperialisms of Germany and Italy, from the Soviet Union, and in Asia, from Japan, and consequently the British had to withdraw themselves from India in 1947. This encounter between the two nations fired the imagination of the writers both Indian and English, and a large body of creative literature came into being.

III
THE CONCEPT OF EMPIRE AND
THE BRITISH RAJ IN INDIA

It is significant to note how creative writers, particularly novelists, played a major role in forming the of India in the minds of the readers alien to Indian socio-political scene. Or according to Dorothy Spencer, the novels and short stories furnish material for a study of the beliefs and ideas regarding the Indian character held by the people themselves. These ideas, closely related to the values and goals of the group as a whole, are often directly expressed in fiction. Or as Oaten puts it,

"New conditions produced new emotions, and new emotions always call for new literary interpretation. And so there grew up in British India a literature, English in form and language, which is unique among the literatures of the world."[6]

Most of the writers, who came to India mainly because of the expansion of British Empire, had in mind the ideology which justified the British presence in India. They interpreted the British Raj from their points of view. It, therefore, becomes more significant, in this context, to examine the concept of Empire in detail. Here one is faced with some crucial problems: is empire a political system in which one group is dominant over others whom it regards as alien and inferior? Or is it some serious, governing philosophy devoted to some noble cause or purpose? Or is it a moral or immoral phenomenon? Taking these problems into account, the philosophers have offered certain theories of imperialism.

Though a number of theories of imperialism have been formulated by various scholars they can conveniently be classified in three main groups. The first group contains economic arguments and often turns around the question: does imperialism pay? Marxist theoreticians have elaborated the economic aspects of imperialism in great detail. They interpret imperialism as a late stage of capitalism when the national capitalist economy has become monopolistic and forced to conquer markets for its overproduction and surplus capital in competition with the monopolistic economies of their capitalist states.

The second group of arguments relates imperialism to the nature of human beings and human groups, such as the states. Such different personalities as Francis Bacon and Adolf Hitler, reasoning on different grounds, nevertheless arrive at similar conclusions. Imperialism to them is part of the natural struggle for survival. Nature has made men unequal, and those endowed with superior qualities are destined to rule others. The third group of arguments is based on moral grounds, sometimes with strong missionary implications. Imperialism is excused as the means of liberating peoples from tyrannical rule or of bringing them the blessings of a superior civilization.

The British Raj in India is a concrete contribution to the development of an imperial theory. In the late Victorian era, many Englishmen held the imperial idea that it was the divine mission of the Anglo-Saxons to civilize the world, 'to bring Asians and Africans the boons, both spiritual and material, of a superior civilization, to establish light, order and law in the dark places'.[7] This view was upheld by most of the theoreticians. The attitude of Sir Francis Younghusband, for example, is as follows:

> No European can mix with non-Christian races without feeling his moral superiority over them.... Our superiority over them is not due to mere sharpness of intellect, but to the higher moral nature to which we have attained in the development of the human race.[8]

Sir Percival Griffith's assessment of the establishment of British rule in India also is similar to that of Younghusband. In his opinion, although European civilization has sometimes been criticised by Indian writers as materialistic, it is, strangely enough, in the realm of ideas that British influence on India has been strongest. The most important illustration of the fact, he believes, is to be found in the development of Indian nationality and the growth of Indian nationalism.[9] Rudyard Kipling, the staunch exponent of the moral superiority of the British, expressed his views in the following poem:

> Take up the White Man's burden
> Send forth the best ye breed
> Go bind your sons to exile
> To serve your captives' need;
> To wait in heavy harness
> On fluttered folk and wild
> Your new caught, sullen peoples,
> Half devil and half child.
> Take up the White Man's burden
> Have done with childish days
> The lightly proffered laurel,
> The easy, ungrudged praise.
> Comes now, to search your manhood
> Through all the thankless years.
> Cold-edged with dear-brought wisdom,
> The judgment of your peers:[10]

A number of British in India were conscious of their imperial mission in India in the Kiplinguesqe manner. Lord Curzon, for example, says in this respect:

> But let be our ideal all the same. To fight for the right, to abhor the imperfect, the unjust, or the mean, to swerve neither to the right hand nor to the left, to care nothing for flattery or applause or odium or abuse - it is so easy to have any of them in India - never to let your enthusiasm be soured or your courage grew dim, but to remember that the Almighty has placed your hands on the greatest of His ploughs, in whose furrow the nations of the future are germinating and taking shape, to drive the blade a little forward in your time, and to feel that somewhere among these millions you have left a little justice or happiness or prosperity.... a dawn of intellectual enlightenment, or a stirring of duty, where it did not before exist - that is enough, that is the Englishman's justification in India.[11]

Though, in this manner, the ideas regarding imperialism were developed, at the turn of the twentieth century the imperial idea started crumbling and the exponents of this idea got disillusioned. Imperialism was severely shaken with the approach of the First World War. The Darwinian theory shattered the belief in the racial superiority of the Europeans which was the most important constituent of the Imperial idea. A new rise of nationalism, and the political and economic evolution of the times are also important causes of the failure of the imperial idea. The idea of imperialism finally collapsed with the Second World War. In India the total failure of the imperial idea resulted in the withdrawal of the British from India in 1947.

Many of imperial ideas mentioned above are concretely evidenced in the Anglo-Indian Literature, especially the novel. Therefore, it is important to have brief note on the tradition of this literature.

IV
BRIEF RESUME OF ANGLO-INDIAN FICTION

The tradition of Anglo-Indian Fiction begins roughly from 1890 and the three decades following this year are especially important as there was the emergence of women authors of light fiction. They were mainly writing romances for the British in England.

Fanny Penny,[12] the first of the early romancers, is a novelist of varied interests. A small group of Anglo-Indian novels is devoted to the life of European and American missionaries in India. Mrs Penny's *The Outcaste* (1912) is an important novel, describing the conversion of Ananda to Christianity and his persecution. What chiefly leads Ananda to Christianity is the death of his friend Coomara at an aviation show and his repugnance towards the Hindu doctrine of transmigration. The remarkable feature of this book is the treatment meted out to Ananda by his friends and relatives. Penny has also paid a considerable attention to the subject of mixed marriages and the problems arising out of them. One of the aspects of the problem of mixed marriages has been discussed in *A Mixed Marriage* (1903). She does not want to prevent such marriages because, in her opinion, they are inevitable.

Penny also depicts the feeling of Indian nationalism in her novels. One of the earlier novels showing the influence of budding Indian nationalism is *The Unlucky Mark (1909)* in which she presents Quinbury, an English sub-magistrate, who condemns the Swadeshi movement of the time. Her other important works are: *The Romance of a Nautch Girl (1898), The Rajah (1911), Love in a Palace (1915) The Romance, The Rajah's Daughter (1921), The Swami's Curse (1922), Magic in the Air (1933),* etc.

The second of early romancers is Alice Perrin.[13] India as a place of vast mysteries and immense horror is the composite theme of her *East of Suez (1901)*, a collection of stories which suggests an obsession with sudden, violent death and sinister disasters. In *The Woman in the Bazaar (1915)* she depicts the tragic story of the pretty, unsophisticated daughter of a country vicar who comes to India as the wife of Captain Coventry. She almost falls a prey to the temptations to which married women are exposed in India, and the jealous nature of her husband forces her to become a woman of the bazaar. The unhappiness of ill-assorted marriages, behind a lightly touched Indian background, forms the subject of her one more important novel, *Government House* (1925). Her other important works are; *Into Temptation (1894), The Spell of the Jungle (1902), Idolatry (1909), Separation (1917), The Vow of Silence (1920), Rough Passages (1926),* etc.

The third important name in this group is B.M. Croker[14] Her account of an encounter of an English woman with an Indian is especially interesting in her books. For example, in *A Family Likeness; A Sketch in the Himalayas* (1901), the heroine, Juliet, who is gathering sticks for a fire while on a hike, comes across a neglected temple surrounded by numerous shrines where she meets a tall, emaciated fakir who had a plan to use the girl as a sacrifice. However, the plan is frustrated by the timely intervention of the hero. *Pretty Miss Neville* (1885) deals with cousins estranged in Ireland but united in India which is full of sensational incidents. Her other important works include *Someone Else* (1885). *Two Masters (1890), Village Tales and Jungle Tragedies (1895), The Happy Valley (1904), A Rolling Stone (1910), In Old Madras (1913), The Pagoda Tree (1919)*, and others.

The fourth novelist, Maud Diver[15] occupies an important place among the novelists of this group. She is interested in the manifold drama of Anglo-Indian life. Though she has no intimate knowledge of the Englishmen in the military stations she has felt for them and dealt with sympathy for them. In *The Great Amulet* (1908), for example, we are introduced to Miss Quita Maurice and Captain Lenox. They separate on the day of their marriage owing to a misunderstanding, but the great amulet of love overcomes their pride and prejudice, steadies them and makes them ultimately realize that marriage is love and comradeship on an equal footing. Her *Lonely Furrow* (1923) deals with the dangers of Indian marriages. Ian Challoner is separated from his wife, Edyth, not only by distance, but by soul and temperament. They are an ill-matched pair. Ian, seeking a cure for his soul-hunger and desparate loneliness in the mountains, discovers in Venessa the ideal mate for him. Her other important works are: *Captain Desmond, V.C. (1907), The Judgement of the Sword (1913), Desmond's Daughter (1916), The Strong Hours (1919), A Wild Bird (1929)*, etc.

I.A.R. Wylie[16] is the last novelist who belongs to the group of early romancers. Published in 1912, *The Daughter of Brahma*, is a phantasmagoric novel about India. Her picture of India was derived entirely from second-hand sources and her lurid imaginings are some indications of the European dream of India as a weird and mysterious place, full of evil spirits. Her other novels are: *The Rajah's People (1910) and Tristram Sahib (1915)*.

The account of these writers demands consideration because, besides their historical importance, they show how the romancers adhered to the bourgeois style of life then current.

The romantic tradition propounded by Penny and others is strengthened by F.A. Steel.[17] Her *On the Face of the Waters* (1896), is, perhaps her best known historical romance. The best parts of the book are those in which the past has been imaginatively recreated - the auction of the property of the deposed King of Oudh, Jim Douglas's romance with Zorabibi and the description of the now almost extinct tribe of the Bunjara. *A Prince of Dreamers* (1908), her second important novel, is an exhaustive study of King Akbar and his dreams of the regeneration of the world, and of creating a united, happy, prosperous India. Steel uses history as a background, as a gorgeous stage, in *The Builder* (1928). The central incident of the story is the great love which is embodied in the Taj. She has reproduced the picture of the desolate soul of the bereaved king with skill and art. It is the humanity of the great Moghul emperors that Steel emphasizes here. Her other important works are: *From the Five Rivers (1893), Tales of the Punjab (189 4), Voices in the Night (1900), The Adventures of Akbar (1913), Mistress of Men (1917), Indian Scene* (1933), etc.

Edmund Candler[18] is another writer of merit. His *The Testimony of Bhagwan Singh*, based upon the tragic love of a Sikh youth for Parbati, the beautiful wife of a goldsmith, shows the author's love for the supernatural. His *Siri Ram, the Revolutionist* (1912), can be regarded as the best of the novels dealing with India's political agitation. Candler describes the book as a transcript from life, 1907-10. His other books are: *The General Plan (1911), and Abdiction* (1922)..

Edward Thompson [9] is another important writer, on India. His *An Indian Day (1927), A Farewell to India (1931) and An End of the Hours (*1938) are structured around his lament for warped relations between the races and his search for a value inhering in the British-Indian encounter. In *An Indian Day* he attempts to interpret and analyse the then political India. His hero, Vincent Hamer, is a young English magistrate who is not enamoured of Indians. But having decided a political case in favour of the Indian accused, he is regarded by his countrymen in India as pro-native. Anglo-India is scandalized and Hamer is transferred to Vishnugram, an untidy mofussil town. He is treated with suspicion by the small group of English residents there while the Indians receive him as an impartial judge. There he meets Hilda Mannering, an independent girl who prefers solitude. Hamer falls in love with her which is requitted only after some time. In *Night Falls on Siva's Hill* (1929), he is contemptuous of a military officer who is forced to lead the life of an exile in the jungles of Trisulbari. The other important works by Thompson are: *Atonement* (1924), *So a Poor Ghost (1933)* and others.

Rudyard Kipling (1865-1936), a writer of great merit, added a new dimension to Anglo-Indian Fiction. Kipling's work related to India is: *Kim*

(1901) *and The Naulakha (*1892) which is written in collaboration with Walcott Balestier. The four volumes, *Plain Tales from the Hills, Soldiers Three and Other Stories, Wee Willie Winkie and Other Stories* and *Life's Handicap,* cover ninety-six stories which have a genuine Indian atmosphere about them and deal with Kipling's own time and people. However, it is in *Kim* that many critics have found Kipling's superb mastery over his Indian material. The journey through the plains and hills of India made by Kim, the Irish orphan reared in the bazaars, and the Lama, a Buddhist monk from Tibet, is treated as a spiritual pilgrimage, In *The Naulakha,* Kipling has given us a conventional account of the palace of the Maharajah of Gokral Seetaram. From the mid-Western American town of Topaz two people with different aims reach India: Kate Sheriff, inspired by a sense of duty to work as a medical missionary among zenana women, and Tarvin, who wishes to marry her, in pursuit of a priceless neckless, the Naulakha. Since Kipling's merits as an artist are great he occupies an important place in the history of Anglo-Indian Fiction.

The publication of E. M. Forster's *A Passage to India* (1924) marked an important development in the field of Anglo-Indian Fiction. It is a cleverly drawn picture of Englishmen in India, a subtle portraiture of the Indian, especially the Moslem mind, and a fascinating study of the problems arising out of the contact of India with the West. In it Forster handles the theme of rape on an English girl by an Indian and creates some immortal characters as Miss Adela Quested, Mrs. Moore, Major Callendar and Dr. Aziz.

After E. M. Forster Paul Scott is, probably, the only Anglo-Indian novelist who has achieved great distinction. His novels make an excellent contribution to the continuation of Anglo-Indian novel tradition since he is the only British writer who deals with the last days of the British Raj with great details. Scott depicts the problems of the British in India who had to face the emergence of nationalism in India - nationalism which saw its culmination between 1942 and 1947. And hence a critical study of his novels becomes imperative in the context of India after decolonization.

NOTES AND REFERENCES

1   E.F. Oaten, *A Sketch of Anglo-Indian Fiction* (London: Kegan Paul,.1908), p. 5.

2   Bhupal Singh, *A Survey of Anglo-Indian Fiction* (London: OUP, 1934), p. 1.

3   John A. Leena Karkala, *Bibliography of Indo-English Literature* (Delhi: Nirmala Sadanand Prakashan, 1974), pp. 4-5.

4   K.R. Srinivasa Iyengar, *Indian Writing in English* (Bombay: Asia Publishing House, 1962), p. 2.

5   H.M. Williams, <u>*Indo-Anglian Literature (1800-1970), A Survey*</u> (Bombay: Orient Longman, 1976), pp. 2-3.

6   E.F. Oaten, *A Sketch of-. Anglo-Indian Fiction.* (London: Kegan Paul, 1908), p. 4...

7   Shamsul Islam, *Chronicles of the Raj; A Study of Literary Reaction to the Imperial Idea Towards the End of the Raj* (London: Macmillan, 1979), p. 2.

8   F.E. Yourighusband, *The Heart of a Continent* (London, 1896), pp. 14-15.

9   S.P. Griffiths, *The British Impact on India* (London: Macdonald, 1952), p. 481.

10 This poem, 'The White Man's Burden', written in 1899 to celebrate the victory of the United States against Spain, which had resulted in the acquisition of Cuba and the Phillipine Islands, appealed the United States to play its part in the imperialist task, quoted from, Shamsul Islam, *Chronicles of the Raj: A Study of Literary Reaction to the Imperial Idea towards the End of the Raj (London: Macmillan, 1979),* p. 6.

11 Lord Curzon, speech in Bombay, 16 November, 1905. Quoted from George Bennett (ed.), *Burke to Atlee, 1774-1947 (London: The Concept of Empire 1953),* p. 105.

12 Fanny Emily Farr Penny, the daughter of a Reverend, married in 1877 the Rev. Frank Penny, a chaplain in Madras. They lived in South India from 1877 until 1901. Mrs Penny wrote some forty-five novels, many of them set in India. She died in 1939.

13 Alice Perrin (1867-1934) was the daughter' of General J.I. Robinson of the Bengal Cavalry and wife of Charles Perrin, M.I.C.E., whom she married in 1886. Perrin spent some years in India when her husband was with the Indian Public Works. She wrote about twenty-five novels and a few collections of short stories many of which were set in India.

14   Bithia Mary Croker, who died in 1920, was the daughter of a Reverend
     and the wife of Lieutenant Colonel John Croker of the Royal Scots and
     the Royal Munster Fusiliers. She spent fourteen years in India and Burma.
     Of her many romances, twenty are set in India.

15   Maud Diver (1867-1945) was born in India. The daughter of Colonel
     C.H.T. Marshall of the Indian Army and the granddaughter of Lord
     Chief Baron Fredrick Pollock, she married Lieutenant Colonel Diver
     when he was a subaltern in the Indian Army. After setting in England
     in 1896 she began writing her novels of Anglo-India and her accounts of
     British heroism in India.

16   I.A.R. Wylie was born in Melbourne, Australia, in 1885 and died in 1959.
     She travelled extensively in Europe but never visited India and the only
     references to India in heir autobiography, *My Life with George* (1940) are
     to her eating Indian food and to her friendship with an Anglo-Indian girl
     whom she had met while they were both at Cheltenham Ladies' College.
     Miss Wylie induced her father to allow her to join this friend for a year
     at a school in Germany.

17   Flora Annie Steel (1847-1929): In 1867, shortly after her marriage, she
     came to India with her husband, a member of the I.C.S. posted to the
     Punjab, and, apart from home leaves, lived there until 1889, making two
     subsequent visits in 1894 and 1898. The years in India entailed the usual
     series of postings, sometimes to remote districts where the Steels were the
     only white people, sometimes to larger stations where they joined in the
     social life of Anglo-India.

18   Edmund Candler, the son of a medical doctor, Candler wanted to be
     a writer and decided on teaching as a career. In 1896 he took a post
     at a school in Darjeeling, during the vacations he travelled in Burma,
     Cambodia and Siam, writing-articles for various Anglo-Indian journals.
     Later on he worked as Professor of English Literature in a college in the
     Madras Presidency and Director of Publicity for the Punjab.

19   Edward J. Thompson (1886-1946), the son of Wesleyan missionary, came
     to Bankura Wesleyan College in Bengal as an educational missionary.
     Between 1934 and 1936 he was Leverhulme Research Fellow at Oxford
     and from 1936 until his death in 1946 he was Research Fellow of
     Indian History at Oriel College. It was after leaving India in 1923 that
     Thompson's efforts on behalf of British-Indian relations were intensified.

CHAPTER II

Theoretical Perspective

I. What is the historical novel?

II. Paul Scott as a historical novelist.

P. A. Attar

WHAT IS THE HISTORICAL NOVEL?

Since there are as many definitions as there are definers I propose to discuss some of the most distinguished critics who have added to the growing corpus of theoretical considerations of the historical novel. According to Paul Liecester, for example, "the historical novel is one which grafts upon a story, actual incidents or persons well enough known to be recognised as historical".[1] In the opinion of John Buchan, "the historical novel is simply a novel which attempts to reconstruct the life and recapture the atmosphere of an age other than that of the writer".[2] Arthur Tourtellot's definition that "the historical novel is simply a reconstruction of some segment of life in the past it creates, it breaths, and it is circumscribed by the small things in the lives of the characters",[3] is much similar to that of Buchan. Avrom Fleishman believes that "the historical novel is a novel which is pre-eminently suited to telling how individual lives were shaped at specific moments of history, and how this shaping reveals the character of those historical periods".[4] Jonathan Nield offers us a definition - "a novel is rendered historical by the introduction of dates, personages or events to which identification can be really given".[5]

Almost all the definitions mentioned above virtually carry no fundamental difference in them since all the critics have accepted that the historical novel should deal with some kind of past. However, to novelize history is such a process which generates a number of issues since the historical novel does not take place by mere placing of historical characters and events together. It is a subtle unification of history and the novel on the basis of artistic qualities; the expression of which appeals to the emotions and intellect of the reader. Or, in other words, we can say that the historical novel is essentially an imaginary narrative of the past in which the historically identifiable dates, events and characters are involved. Perhaps the most inclusive statement, in this context, has been made in *The New Encyclopedia Britannica:*

> The historical novel is a work of fiction that attempts to convey the spirit, manners and social conditions of a past age with realistic detail and fidelity to historical fact. The work may deal with actual historical personages, as does Robert Graves' *I, Claudius* (1934) or it may contain a mixture of fictional and historical characters. It may focus on single historic event, as

does Franz Werfel's *Forty Days of Musa Daqh* (1934), which dramatizes the defense of an American stronghold. More often it attempts to portray *a* broader view of a past society in which great events are reflected by their impact on the private lives of fictional individuals. In the twentieth century, distinguished historical novels such as Arthur Koestler's *The Gladiators (193 4), Zoe Oldenbourg's Destiny of Fire (1960), and* Mary Renault's *The King Must Die (1958)* exemplify an important function of the fictional imagination to interpret remote events in human and particular terms, to transform documentary fact with the assistance of imaginative conjecture, into immediate sensuous and emotional experience.[6]

Taking this comprehensive discourse of the genre into account we can say that the historical novelist, while novelizing history has to work on two levels. On the first, he has to act as a historian and, on the second; as a novelist or a creative artist. In this way, the construction of the historical novel can be studied on the following two levels:

(1) The recreation of the past itself - the recreation of historical atmosphere, collection and selection of historical facts and establishing co-relationship between them.
(2) Transformation of these historical facts into art by weaving and exhibiting the web of human feelings behind them and establishing the artist's point of view towards the facts, the age and its culture.

Thus we can say that the historical novelist is equally concerned with history and the novel. But it must be noted here that the historical novelist, while maintaining the personality of a historian, is basically a novelist, a creative artist and not a historian.

As has been stated earlier, the historical novel does not merely describe the actual historical events as history does. The depiction of historical facts is incidental. The main concern of the historical novelist is not with the actual events, but with the dramatic presentation of them. He tries to recreate a certain period by depicting the emotional character of it. He tries to depict the subtleties of the past human life. In this way, as has been rightly pointed out by H. Butterfield, historical novel is a 'form' of history and not history proper. He says:

> If we find nothing else, we find the sentiment of history, the feeling for the past in the historical novel. On one side, therefore, the historical novel is 'form' of history. It is a w$_a$y of treating the past.[7]

This point is further illustrated by Joseph Turner. He believes that the historical novel as a literary form cannot be characterized by setting out formal elements shared by both the disciplines. Turner explains further:

> First, because there is an inevitable circularity, if not a certain pseudo-empiricism, in such attempts at generic description: isolating common denominators restricts us, by and large, to recapitulating an *apriori* definition. Secondly, because formal properties may not be the genre's distinguishing characteristics: it is the content more than the form, after all, that sets historical novels off from other fiction. Finally, and perhaps most importantly, because the very diversity of the genre frustrates our range to generalize, and condemns our results - should we persist to triviality.[8]

Turner's contribution is important because he has aptly pointed out the autonomy of the historical novel and has shown how it cannot be compared with formal history. However, we must remember that though Turner stresses the content of the novel, the formal categories of the novel are equally important since form and content are not separable from each other.

Now we will turn to the two referents mentioned earlier on which the novelist has to work.

Recreation of the Past

When we say the novelist, like the historian, approaches the past we mean the following things:

1) The nature of historical past
2) Selection and organisation of historical facts

3) Major events and characters chosen by the novelist

4) The degree of documentation as reflected in the novelist's narration.

(1) The Nature of Historical Past

In the theoretical discussion of the historical novel most of the critics have regarded the nature of historical past as an important issue. Various critics have given various opinions regarding the remote and the recent past that the novelist has to choose for his purpose. A.T. Sheppard, for instance, says in connection with the remote past:

> It is comparatively easy to write about the very remote past, to invent names. You may invent names, invent environment, even make your clock strike in Roman halls and years with impunity and with ease - until you found out.[9]

Sheppard's view about the adoption of the remote past for the historical novel to some extent, is right because in the case of remote past where the knowledge of the past is not perfect or not clear the novelist gets full freedom for the play of his imagination. But in such cases, sometimes, there is a risk of the lack of illusion of reality. For example, the novelist who chooses the ancient past as the subject-matter of his novel should necessarily write on the ancient ways of man's life, his fear, love, hatred, conflicts, etc., in an ancient form only. So as to succeed in this matter the novelist must undertake an intensive study of the ancient life. But unfortunately, if the adequate information is not available and if he resorts to too much of imaginative picture there is a danger of the loss of historicity in the novel. Thus, though it is easy to deal with the remote past it is not free from risk.

After this we will examine the views of some of the critics who have opined in favour of the recent past. Ernest Leisy, for example, considers the historical novel a very powerful cultural instrument in the new world since, in his opinion, the other forms like biographical novels, family sagas and regional novels all have merged so variously into historical fiction that border lines are often indistinguishable. He believes that every novel has a 'preterit' quality; hence he defines the historical novel as follows:

A historical novel is a novel the action of which is laid in an earlier time - how much earlier remains an open question, but it must be readily identifiable past.[10]

Daniel Aaron accepts Leisy's concept of "readily identifiable past' and puts forward the idea of 'visitable past' in the following words:

Writers of novelized history are likely to find more popular and lucrative subjects in the "visitable past," to borrow Henry James's term, than in remote times about which most modern readers seem to know or care little.[11]

After stating the nature of the past Aaron shows his concern with the turbulent nature of historical reality when he says that novelized history is likely to be written during the periods of fear and social dislocation when the fictive imagination is susceptible to catastrophe and nightmare. At such times, in his opinion, the writer is encouraged 'to read his own terrors into the cosmos and almost obsessively sniffs the rot and evil of his times'. Not invariably, but, often, the writer will present his 'wasteland' and in the form of black farce as Nathanael West did in his novel of the 1930's Depression, *A Cool Million*, a burlesque on American would-be Hitlers and on the hypocrisy of the American gospel of success.[12] Thus, apart from the insistence on the recent past Aaron's consideration tends, to concern itself with the moral implications of the genre.

Bernard Bergonzi, after Leisy and Aaron, believes in the past of immediate nature when he discusses some of the ways of bringing a sense of history into fiction. In his opinion, novelist's personal experience in some major historical event can be utilised. He states:

There are other ways of bringing a sense of history to fiction.. There are, for example, those distinguished, extended works derived more or less from personal experience in the second World War, like Olivia Manning's *Balkan Tragedy* (1960-65), set in Rummania and Greece, and the late Paul Scott's *The Raj Quartet* (1966-75), set in India.[13]

Thus, so far as the nature of the past is concerned, Leisy, Aaron and Bergonzi believe in the concept of 'immediate or recent past' since they hold that only this kind of past enables us to see to what extent it affects our present.

At this juncture it is significant to study how old the past should be. Brander Mathews, for example, considers the time of the writing of the historical novel important when he says that the really trustworthy historical novels are those which were a-writing while history was a-making'.[14] It means that the historical novel must be written at the time of happening of history. This type of fiction is regarded as contemporary historical fiction by G.M. Trevelyan. He says:

> But there is another class of work which may be called contemporary historical fiction that is epic drama or novel of contemporary manners, which acquires historical value only by the passage of time.[15]

John Marriott, too, has posed the similar problem of time in his book, *English History in English Fiction*, He questions:

> Are there not many novels which at the time when they were written could not be regarded as historical by the mere lapse of time?[16]

But to think in the manner of Trevelyan and Marriott is to create the problem as to what exactly will be the difference between the historical novel and other kinds of novel? Some critics have tried to resolve this problem by giving a certain deadline. Orville Prescott, for example, says:

> An historical novel, according to my personal definition, is any novel in which the action takes place before the author's birth so that he must inform himself about its period by study.[17]

If we regard the time of the writer's birth as a starting point we have to admit that the past may be just two minutes before the writer's birth or a thousand years before that. And the past two minutes before the author's birth will be as important as that of thousand years. Hence, it is very difficult to fix a deadline in this respect. Hence, Prescott's opinion appears to be vague. We will examine the views of a few more critics. Sir Walter Scott, who in theory and practice, laid the foundation stone of the modern historical novel, set -the period of fifty years.[18] Leslie Stephen suggested the period of sixty years in this respect.[19] Leisy, taking the rapid changes in American history into account, regarded the period of thirty-years as a proper lapse in time.[20] In this connection Fleishman says:

> Most novels set in the past - beyond an arbitrary number of years, say 40-60 (two generations) - are liable to be considered historical, while those of the present and preceding generations (of which the reader is more likely to have personal experience) have been called "novels of the recent past."[21]

Mackinlay Kantor argues that contemporaneity cannot be a feature of the historical novel.[22] In his opinion, the distorted imaginative portrayal of a historical fact cannot make the novel historical. The historical novelist must be the history-expert. If he wants to recreate the past by way of a faithful picture of customs, housekeeping, cultural pursuits, wars, conflicts, etc., he must dive deep into the past life. Robert Lively, in this connection, thinks that to be historical, a novel should be laid in a period unfamiliar to its contemporary reader.[23] However, Kantor and Lively do not propose a definite deadline as suggested by Leisy, Fleishman and others.

The above mentioned views bring to our notice that in spite of their efforts to decide how old the past should be the critics have failed to consider the important transitions or landmarks in the process of history, which really becomes a crucial point here. As various transitions are responsible to change the entire character of a certain period, they should be taken as deadlines rather than the birth of the novelist or anything else. In case of the writer who sees the historical change there should not be any bar of time of the writer's birth as such. One thing is strikingly important here that it is not the fundamental question which past should be taken as a base for the historical novel. The question is of novelizing that particular past into an effective and convincing manner.

(2) The Selection of Historical Facts

While novelizing history the main problem before the novelist is that of the selection of facts for his creative purpose. Since the- span of history is very vast it is not only difficult but impossible to novelize the entire span at one place. And hence the selection of historical facts becomes an important issue. History doesn't provide a ready made plot with which he can construct his novel. History consists of a number of events and persons. However, they are so many in number and so widespread that it is very difficult to accept them as they are for the novel writing. In fact, it is the novelist's genius and imaginative power with the help of which the novelist selects from the spread up events and persons, etc., and constructs a novel plot out of them.

The most difficult task, probably, before the historical novelist is that of the selection of proper and useful facts. In this context it is very significant to note Sheppard's views. He says:

> In every period of history, in every episode, in a fragment of stone, in an old weapon, in a name on a desolate grave, in a scrap of verse, is the germ of an historical novel. The difficulty is, or should be, selection. The selection of character and incident is a difficulty. And it is important to know what to reject and what to select.[24]

As far as the matter of selection and omission is concerned we cannot formulate any hard and fast rule as such. It mostly depends on the novelist's discretion and, moreover, on the point of view adopted by the novelist. We will examine the views of some of the critics regarding the selection of material. Some critics believe that it is useful to select only historically important characters and events for the historical novel. Butterfield, for example, says:

> This arena of great 'historic' event provides a more spacious theme for the novelist than mere episodes abstracted from universal history can do. In stead of wandering in the interesting by-ways of the past, and finding surprise of thrilling episode in out-of-the way corners, the novelist may boldly face the full course of important events, and plunge into fate and fortunes of the great, the historical novel then becomes an embodiment of historic things in the sense of far-reaching, loud-sounding issues, and it has a wider canvas, an ampler course.[25]

George Saintsbury, unlike Butterfield, believes that the important historical events are not necessary for the historical novel. He says:

All who have studied the philosophy of novel writing at all
closely know that great historical events are bad subject or are
only good subject on one condition - the steady observance of
which constitutes one of the great merits of Sir Walter Scott.
The central interest in all such cases must be connected with
wholly fictitious personage, or one of whom sufficiently little
is known to give the romancer free play. When this condition
is complied with, the actual historical events may be and
constantly have been used with effects as aids in developing
the story and working out the fortunes of the actors.[26]

The problem cited above, though, to a greater extent, is soundly based, it
does not seem that relevant. The historical novelist aims at the depiction of
the individual and society and the corelation between them in the context of
the chosen historical period. Here incidental events and characters are as much
important as those of the great historical events. In fact, historical events and
characters are not important in themselves, they gain importance only when
they create some issue in the process of history or when they are capable of
stirring the human emotion. In this sense even a minor event may appear
important or a major event may seem meaningless owing to the lack of proper
context. And hence, as the novelist's aim is to recreate the past and make it
alive, whether the events and characters are major or minor, the historical
greatness of events and characters is not as important to the novelist as is the
situation that governs the events. Whether it is a minor or a major event or
character it gets life only with the help of the novelist's genius. In this respect
Fleishman says:

The historical novelist uses the universals of literature -such
categories of aesthetic experience as romance and satire,
tragedy and comedy - to interpret the course of historical
man's career. To portray the interiority of a historical situation
on an invented personage, the novelist thinks of him as a
figure in a universal pattern: not the repetitive patterns of
the philosophies of history, but those of literature. The tragic
or comic, romantic or satiric modes of portraying human
experience in fictional situations have the same universalizing
function when applied to historical situations.[27]

Thus we can say that whatever historical material the novelist selects he should present it through the category of aesthetic recreation.

In respect of the corelation of the historical facts there arises a problem whether the novelist should present them in the context of a particular historical period or a particular phase of that period. In the light of his discretion he can present them in both the forms. Suppose, for example, the novelist has collected the facts regarding the British period of Indian history. If he wishes, in the first place, he can present them against the background of the entire British rule and highlight the socio-economic, political and religious features of Indian society under British regime or, in the second place, he may present them against the background of a particular ruler, for example, India under the rule of Warren Hastings' or Lord Mountbatten, etc. Thus, the novelist can present his facts in both the ways.

(3) Recreation of Socio-Cultural Ethos

The problem of socio-cultural ethos mostly means the recreation of atmosphere and language of the times - atmosphere means the particular way of life, various traditions and socio-economic, political and religious conditions of a certain period. Various historical ages, like the Middle Ages, have their own atmosphere, so have various countries, like England, their own atmosphere. How atmosphere is indispensable to the historical novel is rightly pointed out by Butterfield in the following words:

> Atmosphere, though not merely the result of spontaneity, any more than the electricity is the result of the wire, demands this as its necessary concomitant, as electricity demands the complete circuit. Perhaps it may be said that atmosphere is the result of a conspiracy of details that come in an effortless way from a find that has entered into the experience and made appropriation of the 'world' of some age in history.[28]

Thus, it can be said that a good historical novelist combines the dramatic interest of plot and character with a more or less detailed picture of the varied features of the life of a particular age.

In the creation of atmosphere language plays an important role. Every language carries a cultural matrix which represents the culture of a particular society. According to Mary Lascelles, the problem of language may be initially framed as a question: how should the characters in a tale speak, if we are to suppose they lived in another age than ones, and how should the narrator write, if we are to suppose him their contemporary?[29] Walter Scott gives an appropriate answer to this. He claims that Horace Walpole, in *The Castle of Otranto*, adheres to the sustained tone of chivalry which marks the period of the action. This is not attained by patching his narrative or dialogue with glossarial terms, or antique phraseology, but by taking care to exclude all that can awaken modern association.[30] It means that the novelist should use the language which is suitable to the atmosphere of the age with which he deals. This point is very well expressed by Robert Graves poem:

> To bring the dead to life.
> Is no great magic.
> Few are wholly dead:
> Blow on a dead man's embers
> And live flame will start.[31]

Thus in the creation of an atmosphere the novelist must be certain that his characters think and act in their own time and situation. In their speech or customs or reaction to any situation there must be no hint of changing times or changes in moral values.

(4) The Problem of Historical Accuracy

While considering the point of recreation of the past we must think of the problem of historical accuracy because the subject matter which the historical novelist handles consists of events and changes that actually happened. It has been taken for granted by most of the critics that factuality or fidelity to historical records is an essential of the historical novel, and its characteristic explanations depend upon the degree of factuality of the subject matter. However, the whole problem of factual accuracy as a basis for judgment is altered when the novel, rather than the monograph is concerned. Initially, the novelist appears to have no escape from his primary concern with aesthetic delight. He seeks a wider audience than the historian. Proof of a fact sometimes brings a measure of security to the historian, but the novelist is judged on his ability to make his facts lively. In this respect the creative writer enjoys the basic freedom which is not allowed in the formal historical standards.

At this moment we will examine how critics have opined in this matter. Fleishman, for example, believes that the novelist must maintain the realistic background to the action by adhering to historical facts. He says:

> The historical novel is distinguished among novels by the presence of a specific link to history: not merely a real building or a real event but a real person among the fictitious ones.[32]

Here Fleishman stresses the point that the historical novelist must deal with the actual historical personages against the fictitious background of a historical period.

Doris Marston believes in historical accuracy and says that whatever historic events the novelist uses as the setting for his story he must be accurate in details, in time and in location, but, at the same time makes the novelist aware not to load his story down with too much information.[33]

In spite of maintaining the historical accuracy it can't be denied that the historical novel is a combination of history and imagination, fact and fiction. The problem, however, remains to what extent the novelist should use historical facts and the things created out of his own imagination. This is such a problem, it is true, about which we cannot form any hard and fast rule as such. Where there is adequate information about history available there is, comparatively, a little scope for the novelist's imagination, and *vice versa*. In this case there arises a problem whether the novelist is free to make changes in historical facts. Some critics believe that the historical novel is basically a novel and not history and hence there is no question of maintaining historical accuracy on the part of the novelist. The novelist, therefore, for the sake of his art, can, make necessary changes in historical facts. Unlike this, some critics say that the novelist has no right to make changes in the historical facts. C. Reeve, for instance, says:

> To falsify historical facts and characters, is a kind of sacrilege against those great names upon which history has affixed the seal of truth. The consequences are mischievous; it misleads young minds eager in search of truth, and enthusiasts in the pursuit of those virtues which are the object of their admiration, upon whom one true character has more effect than a thousand- fictions.[34]

In conclusion we can say that though the historical novelist is free to use his imagination he should maintain historical accuracy about the major characters and events which he wants to novelize. Imagination can be used as complementary to history. Suppose if a certain character is proved to be cruel and despotic it will be against history to depict him as a kind-hearted and liberal one. Or it will be anomalous to bring the people of various ages together and depict them as if they belong to one age. The proper use of the imagination will be to consolidate the historical knowledge available in case of characters and events. And it is totally upon the discretion of the novelist to what extent he should use the imagination.

(5) Characterization

The next important point in the recreation of the past is that of characterization. The historical novel is rightly considered to be an aesthetic recreation of the past which involves a more serious aspect of the characters chosen by the novelist. The work of great historical personages is as important as that of laymen. In this context it is significant to note Leisy's view:

> Individuals are more important to him than economic movements of goods or people in the mass. To him the work of women and wood choppers is as significant as that of "military leaders or treaty makers". The every day relations impress him. He dramatizes social processes, that is, as they bear on the life of the individual, and does it with something of the illumination and the emotional power of the poet.[35]

Leisy has made an important statement in this regard in the sense that the novelist's art should not neglect the common people. The life of laymen is regarded as important by him as that of the great men in history; and hence if the historical novel is seen in its totality this point becomes crucial one.

Orville Prescott believes that whether actual historical personages or the entire cast is imaginary is irrelevant. What matters is the all important fact that the author is not writing from personal experience; he is trying to write creative fiction about men and women who lived and loved and died in a world completely different from his own, Prescott thinks that characterization is one of the most difficult of literary tasks. He thinks that the implausibility of the characters is one of the many shortcomings of poor historical fiction. By implausible characters he means that they are either vulgar citizens of the twentieth century masquerading uncomfortably in costume; or they are stiff automations striking attitudes supposed to be appropriate to their time and place. In this connection he says:

> The characters in historical fiction must seem human and interesting; but they must be creatures of their own time, believing many things we no longer believe, feeling, emotions we no longer share.[36]

Thus, a good historical novel is a story about interesting human beings involved in some kind of conflict or significant situation which reveals their characters. In his book, *The Undying -Past,* Prescott illustrates the same point while pointing out the limitations of historians and biographers. He says:

> And so the sense of the past is recaptured through the vicariously felt emotions of historical characters. Historians and biographers can provide facts and interpret events and circumstances. But not even the finest works of history and biography can provide that emotional identification and sense of personal participation which is the special magic of fiction.[37]

Fleishman thinks that the historical novel is pre-eminently suited to telling how individual lives were shaped at specific moments of history, and how this shaping reveals the character of those historical periods.[38] Ernest Baker distinguishes the novelist from the historian on the grounds of characterization when he says:

> To present and interpret facts is the historian's business; to summon up a past epoch, to show men and women alive in it and behaving as they must have behaved in the circumstances, is the labour and joy of the genuine historical novelist.[39]

Thus, characterization is one of the most important features of the historical novel in which the historical novelist observes the concrete possibilities for men to comprehend their own existence as well as the historical forces that affect their lives. He portrays the struggles of history, by means of characters who represent social trends and historical forces. The novelist's greatness lies in his capacity to give living embodiment to the characters he creates. Thus it is possible for him to combine history with genuine human qualities. His characters are not mere representatives of historical movements, ideas, etc. His art consists precisely in individualizing his figures in such a way that the individual traits of characters are brought into a very complex, very live relationship with the age in which they live, with the movements they represent. Thus his characters behave in such a way that is historically authentic.

(6) Documentation

In the context of theoretical framework of the historical novel, the use of documentation made by the novelist figures an important issue. In a way, it makes us think of the writer's concern with the use of various sources available to him. For the sake of convenience the sources of evidence can be placed in one of the following categories:

(a) Documentary sources

The documentary sources of information are those which are contained in published or unpublished documents, reports, statistics, manuscripts, letters, diaries, and so on. These sources are generally divided into primary and secondary sources, Primary sources are those which provide data gathered at first hand. Perhaps the most readily available primary sources are non-literary sources: tombs, old buildings and monuments, towns and cities, artifacts, coins, inscriptions and like. Secondary sources are those which provide data that have been transcribed or compiled from original sources.

(b) Field sources

These sources include living persons who have a fund of knowledge about, or have been in intimate contact with, events and changes over a considerable period of time. These people are in a position to describe not only the existing state of affairs but also the observable trends and significant milestones in historical process. These persons are regarded as 'personal sources' or 'direct sources'. If discretion is used in their selection, various professional and business persons, old residents and community leaders may be utilised as sources of information. Joseph Turner considers this element so important that he gives a distinct category of 'Documented Historical Novel' in his definition of the genre. He observes:

> Generally speaking, then, novels with an actually historical character can be considered historical fiction. Novels of "this type I should like to call documented historical novels, to emphasize their direct link with recorded history.[40]

After the collection of source material the novelist arranges them so that the things he considers most important actually become important in the novel. For this purpose selection of material is essential. The selective decisions the novelist makes determine the nature of the product he creates. If the first function in the historical novel is selective, the second is interpretative. The imagination makes the novelist perceive the significance of facts, penetrate into and beneath them. In this respect it is significant to note the views of Mark Weinstein who emphasises the imaginative element in the historical novel:

> "To stick to facts" now seems meaningless because of the problematic nature of "historical fact". "To show how it really was" is not to produce a photographic copy of an objective reality but to make a leap of imagination.[41]

It is R.G. Collingwood, the British philosopher of history, who has made the most radical contribution to this aspect. He distinguishes between the mere event in history and the thought expressed in it. The processes of history "are not processes of mere events but processes of actions, which have an inner side, consisting of process of thought, and what the historian is looking for is these processes of thought."[42] There is only one way in which the historian can discern the thoughts which he is trying to discover; it is by re-thinking them in his own mind. In this way the historian is his own authority and his thought autonomous and self-authorizing.[43] What gives the historian this authority is his creative or '*a priori*' imagination. Thus a historian is surprisingly like the writer of novels:

> Freed from its independence or fixed points supplied from without, the historian's picture of the past is thus in every detail an imaginary picture, and its necessity is at *every* point

the necessity of *'a priori'* imagination. Whatever goes into it
not because his imagination passively accepts it, but because
it actively demands it. [44]

It is with the help of this *'a priori'* imagination the historian can fill in
the blanks of his narrative. Thus, the historian's narrative is imaginary and in
this sense the writing of the historian, also, is similar to that of the novelist.
In this way, Collingwood suggests that the novelist's act of creation is as valid
and relevant as that of the historian since both offer insights with the help of
'a priori' imagination.

THE NOVELIST'S POINT OF VIEW

In every work of art the artist's point of view is of prime importance.
Apart from the historical interest there is some serious motivation behind the
historical novelist's concern with history. What the historical novelist writes
depends not only on what sort of past he handles, but also on the point of view
he adopts. The following are the novelist's probable aims which guide the act
of his writing:

(i)   novelist's escapist tendency emerging out of his frustration with the
       present world;
(ii)   novelist's consideration of the superiority of the past to that of the
       present world;
(iii) novelist's idea of strengthening the present situation by finding out
       the limitations of the past;
(iv)   novelist's sense of justice regarding the neglected historical figures
       and events;
(v)   novelist's love for nationalism; and
(vi)   novelist's efforts to define the new ways of life in the context of the
       past.

We can say that the novelist's work may reveal one or more than one aims
mentioned above. The novelist reveals his point of view through the selection
of material and the depiction of characters. It is also revealed through the
writer's involvement with the present. The content of the historical novel always
reflects the interests of the age in which it is written. The influence which the

present brings to bear upon the past is of particular importance. It might be called the general ethos of the period in which the novelist is living and writing. Prevailing attitudes, ideas and institutions as well as current events have their influence upon the historical writing. This kind of influence which the present exerts upon the past is a very significant aspect of the historical novel. In this respect R.H. Pearce observes:

> ... historicism assumes that the past, by virtue of its very pastness, becomes an aspect of the present. In effect, a literary work carries the past into the present - and not just as a monument endowed with the sort of factuality from which we may infer its previous mode of existence, but rather as a somehow "Living" thing from whose particularity of form we may apprehend that existence and to a significant degree share in it... however we look toward the past, we cannot free ourselves from the fact that it is somehow here, now, built into our sense of the past.[45]

Thus in showing the relationship between the past and the present the writer inevitably comments on both the past and the present and his commentary reveals his point of view.

Fleishman believes that the historical novel is engaged with the present. He points out that the structural source of the unifying activity of the historical imagination is its dual placement in the past and the present. He says:

> The historical novelist writes transtemporally: he is rooted in the history of his own time and yet can conceive another. In ranging back into history he discovers not merely his origins but his historicity, his existence: as a historical being. [46]

Further, he points out that what makes a historical novel historical is the active presence of a concept of history as a shaping force - acting not only upon the characters in the novel but on the author and readers outside it. In this way, we have to think of the present while arriving at a definite conclusion regarding the point of view of the novelist.

II
PAUL SCOTT AS A HISTORICAL NOVELIST

The consideration of Paul Scott as a historical novelist involves the study of the following issues:

(1) Recreation of the Past

    (a) What is the socio-cultural and political ethos of British India that Scott has recreated?

    (b) What are the major events and changes in 1930s and 1940s that Scott has shown in his novels?

    (c) How has Scott depicted the British and the Indian characters?

    (d) What are the major sources that he has made use of?

(2) Scott' s Point of View

    (a) How Scott's different attitudes towards the British and the Indians establish his point of view?

    (b) How is his point of view revealed through the comparison of the British Raj and the post-Independence Indian period?

(1) SCOTT'S RECREATION OF THE PAST

Paul Scott, who calls the British Raj an 'unexplained ghost'[47] feels it necessary to explain it and describes the phenomenon in the following words:

> Raj, It means rule, it means kingdom, it means the power and the glory of the ruler. To English people it means a phase in their imperial history. To an Indian farmer it used to mean a particular man, the revenue collector.[48]

So far as the recreation of the past is concerned, Scott is seen most powerful and wide-ranging in evoking the complexities of the final years of British domination in India and the effects of its cessation. Since his recreation of the past is that of immediate nature and which is set against the background of the period of turbulance it makes an interesting reading. And moreover, since Scott himself served in the army from 1940 to 1946, mainly in India and Malaya, he could provide the minute details regarding the period on the basis of his own experience in India. At the very beginning of *the Raj Quartet* Scott clearly states his intention which gives the idea about socio-political plight of the British in India:

> In 1942, which was the year the Japanese defeated the British army in Burma and Mr Gandhi began preaching sedition in India, the English then living in the civil and military cantonment of Mayapore had to admit that the future did not look propitious. They had faced bad time before, though, and felt that they could face them again, that now they knew where they stood and there could be no more heart searching for quite a whole yet about the rights and wrongs of their colonial imperialist policy and administration.[49]

From this it becomes very obvious that Scott is more concerned with the life of the British in India than that of the Indians. Among the British in India are regular Indian Army Officers, their wives and children, Indian Civil Service Officers and the missionaries. Scott delineates the events that led the Britishers to introspection and express their melancholic feeling. He has convincingly depicted their sense of rootlessness and alienation as felt by them in India. They are presented with marked despondency as they were then faced with the emerging nationalist movement which made them difficult to continue in India. The second important aspect of the history of this period is Scott's depiction of an infinitely complex Indian society - complexities arising out of its typical social structure, religious beliefs and political ideas. The major events during the period about which Scott writes are: the resignation of the Provincial Governments (1939), the Cripps Mission (1942), the Quit India Movement (1942), the partition of the country in 1947. This is the major historical context in which Scott has set his characters. Among his Indian characters Gandhi is the main figure who represents the Indians' aspiration for self-rule and all others are depicted on the line of Gandhism, except RSS, INA, and Leaguist figures. How Scott is possessed by the British Indian history is expressed in the statement in which he quotes his own words:

> "It released something that I was looking for. I don't know what. I formed a gradual attachment. And after the war an

obsession". Out of this obsession have come eight books set
in India, culminating in an immensely long, very convincing
analysis of a moment of Indian History; four novels on the
end of the British Raj, an extraordinarily ambitious attempt
to recount the events in India between 1942 and 1947, seen
through the eyes of different characters.[50]

In this context it is to be noted that Scott is more interested in the British
characters. He doesn't portray the traditional image of a Sahib created by other
Anglo-Indian writers since he thinks it to be a cartoon image and should be
replaced by a different one. He describes the cartoon image in these words:
"In Anglo-India" surely, the Sahib was shaved while he still slept, then led,
stupefied, to the gusl-khana, folded into his tin-tub, doused, dried, powdered,
dressed, creakily mounted on a no less creaky, stupefied pony, and pointed in
the direction of the daftar (which is Anglo-Indian for office). Arrived there, with
sleep receding and temper rising, he would dock his clerk a week's pay for losing
a file, order four peasants out of his sight, three fined, two rigorously imprisoned,
and one to Districts and Sessions for deportation; and then address himself
to the more agreeable business of writing a sharp minute to the Divisional
Commissioner about the Civil Engineer's plan to drain the marsh out of Burra
for a scheme that would improve agricultural conditions but drive out the
duck and ruin the shooting. Thus kindled for the day, he would return to his
bungalow, riding his pony to a lather of terminal fever, kick the syce in the seat
of his pants for not catching him as the loyal beast fell dead at the foot of the
bungalow steps, then stump up to the verandah in full view of the whole vast
retinue of his servants, but shouting 'Koi Hai[1] in response to some deep reflexive
notion of the protocol to be observed, then clatter into the dark polished dining-
room and sit at the end of the long dark polished table where for a moment he
would be puzzled by the presence of a sour-looking woman reading letters at the
other end of it. Then remembering it was memsahib he would mutter, 'Hullo,
Old thing', and bury himself behind the pages of Civil and Military Gazette."[51]

Scott believes that such an image must be written off for what it is, a
cartoon stuff, and a different one admitted that comes nearer the truth. It is
because, for him, the Britishers' presence in India was altogether a different
phenomenon. In the following words he describes the nature of British presence
in India:

There is something Chekovian about us - and about the
Indians (but that is another story). There is something of the
old Russian landowner, who, burning with reforming zeal,
freed his serfs, parcelled out his land, and then found himself
sitting alone in his study, apparently unoccupied, with all his
good intentions achieved and the splendid echo falling away
into a kind of gravid but unproductive silence.[52]

So in this context the image of a Sahib needs to be changed and to
that extent Scott is right when he thinks of changing it. So far as Scott's
characterization is concerned, he believes that 'you have to get the historical
framework right, so that the action grows both out of the characters and the
pressure of history'. He thinks people in relation to their work more important
than in an ordinary way when he says:

"I believe, because of my temperament and my background, in the
importance of work, naval contemplation bores me. I find work and aspirations
as important to write about as personal problems. There is a bit of the author
in all my characters. But there is also an invisible figure running through it, a
traveller looking for evidence, collecting statements, reconstructing an event.[53]

Scott has recreated all this with his excellent use of various documentary
sources. For example, when he wants to describe the social structure of an
Indian town he selects a town and describes its divisions based on various
castes in India. Or when he wants to describe the missionary work in India
he takes us to a sanctuary and describes its functioning in detail. When he
describes the Jallianwallah Bagh tragedy he relies on the report submitted by
General Dyer after the tragedy. He also makes use of diaries, journals, letters
and various persons to recreate the past. For example, he visits some persons
and makes them talk about the British India which reveals the ethos of the
time. Thus is seen in detail how Scott has recreated the British experience in
India at the close of their rule.

IDEOLOGICAL BACKGROUND

We have seen that Scott's major concern is with the manner in which the
two nations - India and England - fell into confrontation and how the British
rule ended in India. It means Scott is interested in progressiveness of the British
which was not realised due to the process of decolonisation in India. Hence

before we come to the details regarding Scott's point of view we will examine the ideological basis which explains this process.

In his *The Wretched of the Earth* (1963), a classic study of anti-colonialism, Frantz Fanon discusses the plight of the colonized countries under the constant menace of imperialist aggression. Fanon, from the viewpoint of the colonized, exposes the economic and psychological degradation of imperialism. He believes that decolonisation is always a violent process of history. It is the meeting of two forces, opposed to each other by their very nature. The colonial world is a world cut into two - the settler's town and the town belonging to the colonized people. The settler's town is strongly built and brightly lit with the streets covered with asphalt. It is the town of white people, of foreigners.

The town belonging to the colonised people or the native town is a place of ill fame. It is a world without spaciousness. The native town is a hungry town, starved of bread, meat, and light. This world, divided into compartments, is inhabited by two different races. The governing race is of those who come from elsewhere, those, "the others', who are unlike the original inhabitants.

According to Fanon, the settler paints the native as a sort of quintessence of evil. The native society is not simply described as a society lacking in values, but also a society devoid of values. The native is declared as insensible to ethics; he represents not only the absence of values but also the negation of values. In a way, Fanon further points out that the settler dehumanizes the native. He always speaks of the stink of the native quarter, of breeding swarms, of foulness, of gesticulations. And as soon as the native causes anxiety to the settler he points out to him the wealth of Western values. It is to be remembered here that the settler does it consciously to write the history of his own country from his point of view. And because he constantly refers to the history of his mother country, he clearly indicates that he himself is the extension of that mother country. Thus the history which he writes is not the history of the country he plunders but the history of his own nation.[54] The attitude of the settler towards history is cleverly expressed in the following words of Fanon:

> The settler makes history; his life is an epoch, an Odyssey. He is the absolute beginning: 'This land was created by us; he is the unceasing cause 'If we leave, all is lost, the country will go back to the Middle Ages.[55]

Thus, according to Fanon, the settler-native relationship is a typical relationship. The settler puts brute force against the weight of numbers. Colonialism is not satisfied merely with holding a people in its grip and emptying the native's brain of all form and content. By a kind of perverted logic, it, sometimes, turns to the past of the oppressed people, and distorts, disfigures and destroys it. The effect consciously sought by colonialism is to drive into the natives' heads the idea that if the settlers were to leave; they would at once fall back into barbarism, degradation and beastiality.[56] Further, Fanon believes that the colonized man finds his freedom in and through violence. The violence of the colonial regime and the counter-violence of native balance each other and respond to each other in an extraordinary reciprocal homogeneity. Thus, according to Fanon, the process of decolonization concerns inevitably with violence.

Edward Said, in his book, *Orientalism* (1978), develops a subtle and far-reaching critique of the relationship between the West and the East. He believes that this relationship is the relationship of power, of domination, of varying degrees of a complex hegemony [57]. According to Said, being a 'White Man' was an idea and a reality. It meant - in the colonies - speaking in a certain way, behaving according to a code of regulations. It was a form of authority. In various institutions it was an agency for the expression and diffusion of the imperialistic ideas. Being a White Man, in short, was a very concrete manner of a way of taking hold of reality, language and thought.

Such ideas emerge from a very complex relationship between historical and cultural circumstances. For example, one of them is the culturally sanctioned habit of deploying large generalizations by which reality is divided into various collectives: languages, races, types, colours, mentalities, etc. Said thinks that underlying these categories is the rigidly binomial opposition of "ours" and "theirs" with the former always encroaching upon the latter. This opposition is reinforced by anthropology, linguistics and history.[58]

Thus, the studies of Fanon and Said provide us a theoretical paradigm of ideological analysis, indicating its object in the very act of revealing the nature of native-master or colonized-colonizer relationship.

In this way, based on exploitation of natural and human resources of the colonized nation, colonialism perpetuates itself through oppression and aggression. The system, by creating a myth of the colonizer and the colonized, is supported by a social organisation, a government, a judicial system, and an educational pattern. It throws the colonized out of the history making process, calcifies his society and deadens his culture, which in turn, helps maintain the myth of the superiority of the colonizer over the colonized. It further produces a racial culture based on a hierarchical system that attaches importance to distinction of colour, caste, religion, creed and language. In this respect we agree with Prakash Joneja who says: "A distinct mythology, ideology, and philosophy are developed around these distinctions which systematically eliminate a *'raison d'etre*[1] for the colonized whose historical past is distorted, disfigured and finally destroyed if it is not strong enough to hold itself".[59]

One interesting by-product of this colonial relationship is the literature being written by the colonial novelists. This type of literature is wide-ranging and diverse and reflects the changing nature o*f the colonial problem. In the inter-war decades there appeared in the literature of colonialism the relatively new theme of decolonization. In this context my attempt here is to analyse the novels of Paul Scott who figures as one of the most important novelists of the last days of the British rule in India. However, at this moment, before turning to the actual analysis of his novels, we will discuss Scott's ideas regarding the novelist's point of view.

PAUL SCOTT'S POINT OF VIEW

Paul Scott's fiction, since it is essentially an outcome of the extended British colonial power in India, and, since it is wideranging and diverse in nature, reflects the significant aspect of the colonial problem. We can establish Scott's point of view on the basis of his attitude towards Britishers, Indians, British Raj and the Indian government. But prior to that we will examine what his conviction is as the writer's conviction throws light on his point of view. A bit of probing into the views that Scott expresses about his conviction can show us that he only gradually developed certain convictions. Once in reply to his critics who pointed out that he (Scott) seldom repeated himself and that was therefore difficult to define his commitments, he said, "This strikes me as a narrow view. Commitment is for the old and serene. -I am not yet either."[60] And later on he himself talks about his commitment. In a speech made at the Royal Society of Literature he says:

... but the immediate need is to plot the course of my own
Anglo-Indian commitment. There are times when I, even, ask

what on earth I'm upto, writing novels about the declining
days of the now dead British Raj.[61]

It is also relevant at this juncture to examine Scott's outlook on history.
He considers progress in history as a significant aspect:

> If novels were simply sociological reports about people and
> places it would not be awfully wise to write about Anglo-India
> because, discounting the actual progress of history, in that
> restricted sense there's not a great deal to add to *Passage* that
> a modern writer could consider lastingly important to add.[62]

His progressive attitude towards history is also clear when, as has already
been pointed out, he compares the British with the Old Russian landowner
with all his good intentions achieved. A distinction, however, should be made
in the comparison, which is undoubtedly from the landlord's point of view -
though all England's good intentions were not achieved, the British did succeed
to a great extent.

Again it is very important to take into account various ideas that governed
Scott's attitude. At the outset he points out that common to all these ideas
was the idea that the English were 'experts in every practical matter under the
sun: commerce, decent living, law and order, power and politics, to name but
a few'.[63] He believes in the idea of British superiority.

According to him, 'only abroad could an Englishman allow some
consciousness of his superiority to show, and then showing it was a duty;
because abroad the Englishman was an emissary, charged with his country's
trust'.[64] The next important idea Scott believes in is that of paternalism. In
his opinion, 'the product of the Raj was, of course, rule; rule in the form of
benevolent despotism or, as it was called, paternalism, which meant that it
was supposed to be stern but just'. While explaining the idea of paternalism
in connection with the Raj Scott says, "we misjudge its nature if we think of a
bearded patriarchal figure, Bible in one hand and sword in another, ruling the
natives with both. There was, before Mutiny, paternalism of that kind. But it
is not like that now".[65]

Scott's ideas of privilege and integrity play a significant role in defining
the Raj-values. Almost every Englishman in India being a member of the Raj
could enjoy the privileges of it. Scott seems to be very particular about the

idea of privilege since he believes that it is from these privileges, the abuse of them, that the Raj got its bad name. The peculiar quality of privilege is that it can be seen to be enjoyed and seen to be abused. Scott's point is that with the privileges goes responsibility which is overlooked by the Indians and only the abuses are pointed out. Or that though the Englishmen enjoyed privileges they were always conscious of moral integrity in their character; integrity meant the incorruptibility of man's whole being in relation to the job he was doing.[66] It became a passion, an obsession. It was possibly the one part of the product that stood the test of time, of history, of affairs. One more important idea in this respect was the belief that the Raj held the balance of power between otherwise irreconcilable forces that would lose no opportunity to cheat, to threaten or slaughter one another. The Raj always said it had united India. It had in the sense that it imposed a single rule of law upon all its people.[67] Thus it is in the context of various explanatory ideas Scott has projected the image of an Englishman as a superior being.

The above mentioned ideas regarding the Englishmen in India are substantiated when we take Scott's ideas about India and the Indians into account. He calls India a land of deafening noise and intense melancholy and silence. It seems to him to have no echo.[68] While commenting on the general nature of the Indians he says that Indians revere the insane. He also believes that "the Indians have almost no sense of history and no great interest in future, and that this again is the result of a rigid caste-system and a religious attitude to the life they are presently living as being a mere stage on the road to nowhere"[69] In India, he believes, "there were corruption, bribery, false witnesses, a wild and irritating inability to do even the simplest thing right first time (i.e., the English way), endless arguments, open emotionalism, revolting personal habits, noise, squalor, filth, religious begotry, idol worship, ghastly practices, fawning, flattery, terrible cheek and sullen insolence. What could be worse?"[70]

Further, he believes that the Indians always talk about the bad side of the British and don't recognise the value of the responsibility borne by the British. Scott doesn't like that "any middle-aged or elderly Indian will have a tale to tell of being cold shouldered, insulted, thrown out of a first-class compartment on the Frontier Mail, kept waiting on a verandah, pushed out of the way in post office, refused admission to a club", etc. He is also critical of the way in which the Indians were anglicised.[71] He holds that their anglicisation was being shaped in a wrong way because it was fed with the ideas that questioned the values of the Raj. Finally, he says, "the political impasse between the Muslims arid the Hindus during the negotiations for British withdrawal and the bloody events that accompanied the birth of the two independent dominations of India and Pakistan, seemed to prove that the Raj had been right all along". He feels that the partition was not a right thing, because "the Indians were still incapable of correct (i.e., English style) government".[72]

Lastly, we will see how Scott's comments on the British Raj and the Indian government substantiate his point of view. In some of his novels Scott has referred to India in the sixties and seventies which enables him to relate the Raj to the present day Indian situation. Commenting on the post-Independence Indian scene, he says that "the world for which 'the Raj prepared and conditioned India is not the one in which she struggles". Or, he says, "If you speak to an Indian farmer today and he is middle-aged he may well recall the time when Collector Sahib was an Englishman. If he is quite elderly he will- almost certainly be able to do so and then, if you are English yourself, he will probably say that things were better in those days."[73]

These ideas which lie explanatory at the centre of Scott's novels clearly point out that Scott looked towards the final years of the British in India from the British point of view only, which, he believes, was progressive. What Jean Zorn thinks of him is right:

> Paul Scott shares with Tusker Smalley a look of wearied but unmistakable Englishness. Scott has retired from a number of occupations, but the colonial service is not among them.[74]

NOTES AND REFERENCES

1   Earnest E. Leisy, *The American Historical Novel* (Norman: Univ. of Oklahama, 1950), p. 4.

2   Reproduced from Sir J. Marriott, *English History in English Fiction* (London: Blakie and Son, 1940), p. 2.

3   Arthur B. Tourtellot, "History arid the Historical Novel", *Saturday Review*, 23 April 1940, p. 16.

4   Avrom Fleishman, *The English Historical Novel: Walter Scott to Virginia Woolf* (Baltimore and London: Johns Hopkins Press, 1971), p. 10.

5   Jonathan Nield, *A Guide to the Best Historical Novels and Tales* (New York: Burt Franklin, Reprint, 1968), p. XVIII.

6   *The New Encyclopaedia Britanica*, p. 64.

7   H. Butterfield, *The Historical Novel* (Cambridge: Univ. Press, 1924), p. 2.

8   Joseph Turner, "The Kinds of Historical Fiction: An Essay in Definition and Methodology," *Genre* (12:3, 1979), p. 337.

9   A.T. Sheppard, *The Art and Practice of Historical Fiction*, p. 116, Reproduced from Govindji, Hindike Aitihasik Upanyasonmen Itihas Prayoqa (Meerut: Kalpana Prakashan, 1974), p. 153.

10   Ernest Leisy, *The American Historical Novel* (Norman: Univ. of Oklahama Press, 1950), p. 5.

11   Daniel Aaron, "Fictionalizing-the P$_a$st," *Partisan Review* (vol. XLVII, No. 2: 1980), p. 231.

12   *Ibid.*

13   Bernard Bergonzi, "Fictions of History," Malcora Braaouty and David Palmer (ed.), *Stratford. Upon-.Avon Studies*, 18 (London: Arnold Hienemann, 1979), p. 54.

14   Brander Mathews, *The Historical Novel and Other Essays* (1901), Reproduced from Govindji, p. 101.

15   G.M. Trevelyan, "History and Fiction," Clio, *A Muse and Other Essays* (London: Longmans, 1934), p. 93.

16   Sir J. Marriott, *English History in English Fiction* (London: Blakie and Sons, 1940), p. 3.

17   Orville Prescott, *The Undying Past* (New York: Doubleday and Co. Inc., 1961), p. 16.

18 Ernest Leisy, *The American Historical Novel* (Norman: Univ. of Oklahama, 1950), p. 5.

19 A.T. Sheppard, *The Art and Practice of Historical Fiction*, p. 16, Reproduced from Govindji, p. 102.

20 Ernest E. Leisy, *The American Historical Novel* (Norman: Univ. of Oklahama) p. 3.

21 Avrom Fleishman, *The English Historical Novel: Walter Scott to Virginia Woolf* (Baltimore and London: Johns Hopkins Press, 1971), p. 3.

22 Mackinlay Kantor, "The Historical Novel," Irving Stone et al., *Three Views of the Novel*, Lectures presented under the auspices of the Gertrude Clarke Whittal Poetry and Literature Fund, Reference Department, Library Congress, Washington, 1957, p. 31.

23 Robert Lively, *Fiction Fights the Civil War: An Unfinished Chapter in the Literary History of the American People* (Chapell Hill: The Univ. of North Carolina Press, 1957), p. 19.

24 A.T. Sheppard, *Art and Practice of Historical Fiction*, p. 85, Reproduced from Govindji, p. 152.

25 H. Butterfield, *The Historical Novel* (Cambridge: Univ. Press, 1924), p. 67.

26 George Saintsbury, Reproduced from Govindji, p. 155.

27 Avrom Fleishman, *The English Historical Novel: Walter Scott to Virginia Woolf* (Baltimore and London: Johns Hopkins Press, 1971), p. 8.

28 H. Butterfield, *The Historical Novel* (Cambridge: Univ. Press, 1924), p. 106.

29 Mary Lascelles, *The Story-teller Retrieves the Past: Historical Fiction and Fictious History in the Art of Scott, Stevenson, Kipling and Some Others* (Oxford: Clarendon Press, 1981), p. 136.

30 *Ibid.*

31 Reproduced from Peter Green, "Aspects of the Historical Novel", Peter Green (ed.) *Essays By Divers Hands: Being the Transactions of the Royal Society of Literature*, New Series, Vol. XXI (London: OUP, 1962), p. 53.

32 Avrora Fleishman, *The English Historical Novel: Walter Scott to Virginia Woolf* (Baltimore and London: Johns Hopkins Press, 1971), p. 4.

33 Doris Marston, *A Guide to Writing History* (Cincinnati OH 45242: Writer Digest Div. F. & W. Corpn. Publishing, 1976), p. 103.

34 C. Reeve, Reproduced from Govindji, p. 17 4.

35 Ernest E. Leisy, *The American Historical Novel* (Norman: Univ. of Oklahoma), p. 6.

36 Orville Prescott, *In My opinion: An Inquiry into the Contemporary Novel* (New York: Charter Books, 1963), p. 134.

37 Orville Prescott, *The Undying Past* (New York: Doubleday & Co. inc., 1961), p. 17.

38 Avrom Fleishman, *The English Historical Novel: Walter Scott to Virginia Woolf* (Baltimore & London: Johns Hopkins Press, 1971), p. 10.

39 E.A. Baker, *The History of the English Novel*, Vol. VI (New York: Barnes & Noble Inc., 1929, rep. 1969), p. 135.

40 Joseph Turner, "The Kinds of Historical Fiction: An Essay in Definition and Methodology", *Genre* (12:3, 1979), p. 337.

41 Mark Weinstein, "The Creative Imagination in Fiction and History," *Genre* (9:3, 1976), p. 264.

42 R.G. Collingwood, *The Idea of History* (London: OUP, 1964) p. 215.

43 *Ibid.*, p. 236.

44 *Ibid.*, p. 245.

45 Roy Harvey Pearce, *Historicism Once More: Problems and Occasions for the American Scholar* (Princeton: Princeton Univ. Press, 1964), p. 5.

46 Avrom Fleishman, *The English Historical Novel: Walter Scott to Virginia Woolf* (Baltimore & London: Johns Hopkins Press, 1971), p. 5.

47 Paul Scott, "The Raj," Frank Moraes and Edward Howe (ed.), *India* (Delhi: Vikas, 197 4), p. 72.

48 *Ibid.*

49 Paul Scott, *The Jewel in the Crown* (Frogmore: Panther Books Ltd., 1966), p. 10.

50 Caroline Moorehead, "Novelist Paul Scott: (Setting Engrossed in the Death-Throes of the Raj," *Times*, October 20, 1975, n. pag.

51 Paul Scott, "India: A Post-Forsterian View," Mary Stocks (ed.), *Essays* By Divers Hands (London: OUP, 1970), p. 116.

52 *Ibid.*

53 Caroline Moorehead, "Novelist Paul Scott: Getting Engrossed in the Death-Throes of the Raj," *Times*, October 20, 1975, n. p.

54 Frantz Fanon, *The Wretched of the Earth* (Harmondsworth: Penguin, 1963), p. 40.

55 *Ibid.*

56 *Ibid.*, p. 169.

57 Edward Said, *Orientalism* (London & Henley: Routledge and Kegan Paul, 1978), p. 5.

58 *Ibid.*, p. 227.

59 Om Prakash Joneja, *Colonial Consciousness in Recent Black American*, Indian and African Fiction with Special Reference to the Novels of Richard Right, Ralf Ellison, James Baldwin, Raja Rao, R. K, Narayan, Mulk Raj Anand, Chinua Achebe, T.M. Aluko and James Ngugi, A Ph.D. Thesis submitted to the Maharaja Sayajirao University of Baroda, August 1980, p. I.

60 John Wakeman (ed.), *World Authors: a Companion Volume to Twentieth Century Authors* (New York: The H.W. Wilson Co.', 1975), p. 1270.

61 Paul Scott, "India: A Post-Forsterian View," Mary Stocks (ed.). *Essays By Divers Hands* (London: OUP, 1970), p. 114.

62 *Ibid.*, p. 117.

63 Paul Scott, "The Raj," Frank Moraes and Edward Howe (ed.) *India* (Delhi: Vikas, 1974),

64 *Ibid.*, p. 75.

65 *Ibid.*, p. 77.

66 *Ibid.*, p. 83.

67 *Ibid.*, p. 85.

68 *Ibid.*, p. 70.

69 *Ibid.*, p. 71.

70 *Ibid.*, p. 76.

71 *Ibid.*, p. 84.

72 *Ibid.*, p. 85.

73 *Ibid*p, p. 72.

74 Jean G. Zorn, "Talk With Paul Scott,' *New York Times*, August 21, 1970, p. 37.

CHAPTER III

Pre-*Raj Quartet* Novels

1. *THE ALIEN SKY*

The Alien Sky (1953)

The genesis of the theme of *The Raj Quartet* - relationship between Indians and British in the historical context - can be traced in *The Alien Sky*, Scott's belief that the British were morally superior to the Indians in the sense that they were conscious of their integrity and were fully committed to their work is revealed for the first time in the present novel.[1]

The novel is set in the cantonment of Marapore. It is June 1947, the month in which the British were told that the ruling power would be transferred to the Indians in two months. They have an unexpectedly short time to make their future plans. There are the persons like army widow, Cynthia Mapleton, an archetypal memsahib who wishes to go to Kenya where white supremacy still reigns, Tom Gower, a liberal Englishman who edits the local newspaper and runs an experimental farm in the nearby hills. His wife, Dorothy, is on severely strained relations with him. There are also the persons like the young American Joe MacKendrick, the elderly spinster, Harriet Haig, ex-governess to the Prince of Kalipur and the Indians like Mr. Nair, the owner of the local newspaper and the farm of Ooni and the young fanatic revolutionary named Vidyasagar.

In recreating the image of India Scott revokes the atmosphere of the times which, according to Butterfield, is a necessary concomitant of the historical novel.[2] The image of India as depicted by Scott in this novel shows his belief that it is the land of the people incapable of correct government, the people, unlike British, lacking in ability to rule themselves.[3] Naturally, it leads to his belief that only the British could do something progressive in India. While pointing out the backwardness of India he thinks of Calcutta where 'the hotel floors were tiled and where the bathroom was more than a prison cell with a zinc tub, more than a dim place haunted by grotesque spiders which raced across the duckboards from beneath the wooden doors'.[4] Or it can also be found when he says that in India 'the emotions were always subject to shock. Behind beauty was ugliness'.[5] The heat and dust in India is described by Scott when MacKendrick notices:

> (he noticed), passing on his way the lumbering ox-carts which the drivers guided through the sand-like dust by twisting the tails of the white, humped oxen harnessed on either side of the single shafts.

> The heat had oppressed him for he had not accepted it
> The old Indian, asleep on a charpoy in the shade of the peepul
> trees, the single files of women, dressed in unlovely, magenta
> coloured sarees, walking purposefully for nothing to nothing,
> the naked children.., all these had accepted it, seemed content
> to be exhausted by it.[6]

The heathenism in India is also referred to when he says that 'the strange fear of gods and devils is always at work under India's skin.'[7] India's poverty is described symbolically in the person of Steele's Indian woman who had the 'pitifully thin hands, the bowed head, the kneeling, shrouded figure, the bare calloused feet - all the poverty and wretchedness that was India'.[8] The non-academic atmosphere in Indian education institutes is pointed out when he describes the Laxminarayan Memorial College as 'riddled with politics'.[9] About the Indians he says, 'they can't stop gossiping, they know everything we do, and what they don't know they make up.'[10]

Thus, the image of India as depicted by Scott in this novel is not fundamentally different from that of Rudyard Kipling who considered it a land of 'half devil and half child'.[11] This clearly points out Scott's British outlook towards India. This image, which we find fully developed in his *magnum opus, The Raj Quartet*, is nicely fitted with the British image of mature, rational leader of father figure who was needed to take care of the child. In this respect it is significant to note how he creates the British characters. Here we learn that he has presented them in such a manner that we feel they are simply inseparable from the historical process and in doing so he illustrates Baker's point that:

> ... to summon up a past epoch, to show men and women
> alive in it and behaving as they must have behaved in the
> circumstances, is the labour and joy of the genuine historical
> novelist.[12]

In this context the predicament of Tom Gower becomes an important point of reference. Tom Gower, a liberal Englishman who is committed to the job of reforming India, is unwanted by the Indians at the eve of Independence. The nature of his commitment is now revealed as dependent upon the continuing goodwill of Indians and suddenly that goodwill no longer seems certain.

While depicting the character of Tom Gower Scott also presents the Indians like Vidyasagar whose whose extreme incompatibility with the British is pointed out. How in spite of his liberal attitude Gower is not accepted by the Indians is described at one of the functions at the Laxminarayan Memorial College. After the sports event in the college was over Gower was invited to distribute the prizes to the winners. Vidyasagar, a young boy of sixteen years was one of the prize-winners. When Vidyasagar's turn came Gower took the large silver cup and held it out to Vidyasagar. But instead of taking it the boy turned on his heel and marched back along the way he had come. Afterwards he was taken away in procession borne by two youths and the others holding a banner with the inscription, "India for Indians".[13] Later they went to the offices of the *Marapore Gazette* and painted the words, "Go Home Gower".[14] Scott is critical of this anti-British demonstration because the Indians were asking the same Tom Gower to go back to England who had done a lot of good for the Indians. His commitment to the job is to be noted in the following words:

> Tom Gower is a name not unknown, you see. He is in India
> many years and takes our problems to heart.[15]

Tom is not only insulted in the college by a young man like Vidyasagar but he is also insulted by an elderly person like Nair who asks Tom to resign his editorship of the *-Marapore Gazette* because he thought he did not reflect the Indian feelings through his articles in the Gazette.

This image of Indians is further recreated when Steele, Gower's assistant at Ooni, is shot dead by Vidyasagar who held Steele responsible for the killing of Bholu, Mackendrick's Indian servant. In this respect it is to be noted how Scott has depicted Vidyasagar as a person who does not have a sense of justice. When he was imprisoned after the murder of Steele, Gower went to see him and made him aware of the punishment he would get for the crime. But Vidyasagar, unmindful of that, said:

> You are wrong, Mr Gower. It will be many days, many weeks,
> many months, before the trial takes place. By that time the
> British will not be here, and I will have justice."[16]

Here Scott points out that Vidyasagar does not feel anything for the murder of Steele. He also means to say how Indians are not fit for self-rule because if they are granted it the persons like Vidyasagar would become free and thus they would take an- undue advantage of the self-rule. On the contrary, the British are shown to be the persons quite conscious of integrity. In showing that in spite of their rule, unlike Indians, they are always aware of the sense of justice irrespective of the person being English or Indian. This is illustrated in the case of Bholu who was killed by Steele. Even though the killer is an Englishman they do not neglect the case is evident in the following words of Mr Forster, the District Magistrate of Marapore:

> That it's possible the population turn round and say we're closing a blind eye to a killing because the man with the gun was British and the man with the bullet in his guts was Indian.[17]

This point is further illustrated when he says that by dragging Steele into the court of law they are going to prove the honesty of the British. He, therefore, says:

> Leave things as quiet as we can. Forlorn hope. But there's no reason why we shouldn't give them another example of the incorruptibility of British justice.[18]

Thus, despite the fact that the British were quite capable of ruling the country, the forces of Indian national struggle made it extremely difficult for the British to do so. Their leaving India is described thus:

> They were stubborn, these Britishers on the point of departure, stubborn like the aged and the dying. About them was the smell of decay, the smell of sickroom. They were clearing out of India and leaving the smell behind them. If you sniffed, now, it smarted in your nostrils. Decay. Death. An end to ambition. A burial of pride.[19]

Here Scott aims at saying that in spite of their good work in India they couldn't get respectable valediction which shouldn't have happened. And the reason that he advances for this is their inability to understand the nationalist forces which didn't recognise the worth of the British Raj. Hence Gower says:

I think if we're to blame for anything in the years we've ruled it's our failure to understand these forces even at the moment of departure.[20]

How the historical changes affect the persons can also be seen in the character of Miss Harriet Haig, one time governess of the Maharajah of Kalipur. With the British withdrawal from India the princely thrones tottered and the States had been deserted. It affected the lives of the British who served the princes. Harriet's feeling of this effect is recorded in the following words:

> "And suddenly she saw herself as an old woman sitting foolishly on the verandah of an almost deserted club. She could hear its silence and across its silence the echo of someone saying: Our lives are bloody well messed up and our occupations gone. Around her in the emptiness were voices, voices which betrayed the anguish there was in being forced to hand on to what was already moving away, because there seemed to be no other support.[21]

Apart from the tragic life of the British at the eve of Independence, what Scott is seriously occupied in this novel is the problematic life of the Eurasians or Anglo-Indians. He considers it a serious problem because the Eurasians were considered as 'social pariahs' in India.[22] Patrick Swinden, who considers the Eurasian subject of fundamental importance, says that the British withdrawal made them fearful of what the future might hold for them.[23] To be an Anglo-Indian was considered as a slur which can be seen in the character of Dorothy Gower, Tom's wife. Because of the forced marriage there was strained relationship between Tom and his wife Dorothy. Her uncommunicativeness with everyone around her is inseparable from the strain involved in her pretension to English birth and upbringing and the hatred she feels towards her Indian homeland. She is afraid of getting exposed of her Anglo-Indian identity. And it is because of this only she is not willing to go to England with Tom and therefore it can be said that Tom Gower is a victim of Dorothy's Eurasian identity.

As rightly pointed out by Swinden, certainly the most powerful scenes in this novel have 'to do with the treatment of Eurasians by members of the white community.[24] The first of these describes a party at which Judith Anderson's pretensions to having been brought up in Brighton are cruelly exposed by Cynthia Mapleton. The second is at the end of the book when MacKendrick, about to make love to Dorothy, accuses her of deceiving Gower for inadequate and totally sadistic reasons. Dorothy's predicament draws our attention when she says that it is impossible for her to live with Tom by revealing her identity. She, therefore, says:

> I can stay with him in Kalipur so long as he never knows about me. I think I can live with him in Kalipur and not mind. Exist, not live. I've lost that chance, or never had it. Which, I wonder? And Kalipur won't be like Marapore, or Calcutta, or Lahore. It won't be British India. That's all in the past, it's all going into the past. If I went to England I'd be going with it, taking it with me. I can't do that, not with Tom. Tom mustn't know.[25]

The fact that the British do not treat Eurasians as their equals speaks of their belief in the racial superiority. Thus, most of the characters in the novel illustrate how the historical event of Independence affected their personal lives and governed their destinies.

Perhaps, it being Scott's early historical novel, he is not seen as mature in his art of creative writing as is seen later in *The Raj Quartet*. And, therefore, perhaps, the book is not well received by the critics. For example, *The Times Literary Supplement* reviewer calls it a 'less satisfactory book'[1] because, in his opinion, 'it is a pity that Mr Scott has used an improbable central incident in the story - a young American businessman named MacKendrick who is trying to solve psychological difficulties of his own by coming out to see the woman who has been his dead brother's mistress.[26] Or Derwent May says that 'when Mr Scott stirs about in the subconscious of the Anglo-Indian women he is not entirely at ease and the American visitor is a rather contrived and sketchy figure.[27] Similarly, John Metcalf criticises it for it lacks a focal point.[28] However, in spite of its shortcomings the importance of the novel cannot be denied since in it we find the genesis of *The Raj Quartet*.

NOTES AND REFERENCES

1   Paul Scott, "The Raj", Frank Moraes and Edward Howe (ed.) *India* (Delhi: Vikas Publishers, 197 4), p. 83.

2   H. Butterfield, *The Historical Novel* (Cambridge: University Press, 197 4), p. 106.

3   Paul Scott, "The Raj", Frank Moraes and Sdward Howe (ed.) *India* (Delhi: Vikas Publishers, 1974), p. 85.

4   Paul Scott, *The Alien Sky* (London: Hienemann, 1967), p. 11.

5   *Ibid.*, p. 13.

6   *Ibid.*, p. 14.

7   *Ibid.*, p. 237.

8   *Ibid.*, p. 253.

9   *Ibid.*, p. 20.

10 *Ibid.*, p. 138.

11 This image of India is described by Rudyard Kipling in his poem, 'The White Man's Burden"[1] which was written in 1899 to celebrate the victory of the United States against Spain.

12 E.A. Baker, *The History of the English Novel*, Vol. VI (New York: Barnes & Noble Inc., 1929, rept. 1969), p. 135,

13 Paul Scott, *The Alien Sky* (London: Hienemann, 1967), p. 54.

14 *Ibid.*, p. 55.

15 *Ibid.*, p. 60.

16 *Ibid.*, p. 255.

17 *Ibid.*, p. 233.

18 *Ibid.*, p. 234.

19 *Ibid.*, p. 67.

20 *Ibid.*, p. 193.

21 *Ibid.*, p. 47.

22 *Ibid.*, p. 36.

23 Patrick Swinden, *Paul Scott; Images of India* (London: Macmillan, 1980), p. 19.

24 *Ibid.*, p. 23.

25 Paul Scott, *The Alien Sky* (London: Hienemann, 1967), p. 206.

26 Review of *The Alien Sky* by Paul Scott, *Times Literary- Supplement,* September 25, 1953, p. 609.

27   Derwent May, rev. of *The Alien Sky* by Paul Scott, *New Statesman and Nation*, October 17, 1953 (46: 46 2).

28   John Metcalf, rev. of *The Alien Sky* by Paul Scott, *Spectator*, September 25, 1953 (190: 338).

2. *THE BIRDS OF PARADISE* (1962)

The Birds of Paradise (1962)

In both the pre-*Raj Quartet* novels, *The Alien Sky*, and *The Birds of Paradise*, Scott makes an important statement regarding the British Indian history which gets an elaborate expression *in The Raj Quartet*: since the Indians were incapable of ruling their nation, the world for which the Raj prepared India is not one in which she struggles to survive.[1] It clearly defines his attitude towards the British Indian history which has got the underlying idea of the superiority of the British.

As pointed out by Patrick Swinden, *The Birds of Paradise* 'is almost certainly Scott's finest pre-*Raj Quartet* achievement.[2] The novel, though contemporary in tone, recreates the history of British India through an exercise in memory, the technique that he adopts in some of his later novels, especially, *The Jewel in the Crown* (1966) and *Staying On* (1977).

William Conway, about forty five, who is a prosperous but unhappy London executive, has taken a sabbatical year and is spending it on a tropical island called Manoba. In the same year he visits India in a, to use the author's words, 'fit of pique'.[3] The protagonist, William Conway, who has spent his youth as a son of an official in one of the princely states of India, is remembering things past and writing his memoirs down. It is mainly through these memoirs that Scott has recreated the British Indian history in this novel. The protagonist's strong concern with the past becomes explicit in the following lines when he states:

> I hadn't killed the past by going back to Jundapur. I hadn't
> buried my dead. The dead weren't dead. Everything had grown
> directly out of the past, undeviatingly; you could squint from
> the rather blowsy flower down the stem and see the living root;
> a root' which had shaped me to want to ride against the wind
> but also shaped me to drift with it until it left me in a place
> like Four Birches with Anne.[4]

The recreation of the past in this novel revolves around the following aspects of the British Indian history: (i) the life of the Indian princes and their relationship with the Crown, (ii) the formation of the Indian National Army and the treatment given to the British Prisoners of War by the Japanese in the Second World War.

First we will see how Scott has recreated the lifestyle of Indian princes through the *tableaux vivant* from Tradura to which all Conway's major boyhood recollections belong. The recreation of the life style becomes significant from the point of view of atmosphere, which, according to Butterfield, means the particular way of life of the people of a certain historical period, various traditions and socio-economic and political conditions of an age and is a necessary concomitant of a historical novel.[5] The most important event that Scott has described in this respect is that of the 'royal shikar', one of the off-duty pursuits of the Raj as described by Charles Allen. Allen, in his book entitled, *Raj: A Scrapbook of British India* (1877-1947), records that the practice of slaughtering large number of tigers and bears and even large number of lesser game animals and birds - wild duck and sand-grouse, in particular - was confined to the Native States and quite a number of princes devoted their energies to organising immensely elaborate camps and schools, to which they invited Viceroys and Governors and lesser Europeans whenever possible. He further states that it would be wrong to think of them as sporting occasions; they were an essential part of the rituals of state, necessary displays of power by princes made largely impotent by the *Pax Britanica*.[6] One such shikar (animal hunt) conducted by Ranjit Raosingh, the Maharajah of Tradura, is described by Scott in such an elaborate manner that it becomes one of the major issues of the novel. He describes the shikar of the Kinwar tiger quite minutely. When the tiger appeared in 1929 the people were convinced that it had turned man-eater. A petition for shikar was fixed for the beginning of March and old Ranjit Raosingh decided to conduct it with all the pomp and display at his command. Then Scott goes on describing in detail how the shikar was conducted in a royal manner. Here the image of the prince as depicted through the event of shikar is the image of a benevolent ruler. How the shikar was common in Indian princely states can also be gathered from Manohar Malgonkar's *The Princes*. The Maharajah, as depicted by Malgonkar, went tiger shooting and in the traditional manner arranged all the paraphernalia which went with "bagging" a tiger. He invited British officials to join him in the hunt and disposed of the 'bagged' tigers generously among his guests. Though Malgonkar sympathises with the princes he, at the same time, points out their negligence of the development of the states. He therefore, says:

> Processions, military parades, durbars and other forms
> of pageantry left little time or money for hospitals or

road-building, and the industrial age was kept at bay as something alien, an imposition from the West.[7]

As far as the event of Shikar is concerned, though Scott has depicted the princes as benevolent he has also, like Malgonkar, criticised them at some places.

The historical novel, according to Fleishman, tells how individual lives are shaped at specific moments of history[8] and how, according to Prescott, an individual is a creature of his own time, believing things we no longer believe.[9] Here the character of William Conway is a point of reference, it is to be seen how his personality was shaped in the Indian state of Tradura, how he was treated by the Indian prince and how he was kept away from the native influence by his father. William Conway was born in India at the Residency in Gopalkand in 1919, when his father was acting as assistant to the Resident. The fact that the fireworks were ordered at the time of his birth by the ruler of Gopalakand, the Maharajah, Sir Pandirakkar Dingit Rao, known to the English as Dingy Row, proves how the British were respected by the Indian princes. Again the whole description of the reception ceremony at his birthday also speaks of the same. Later on they moved to Pankot and then to Tradura to which nearly all William's major boyhood recollections belong.

William's father probably distrusted the influence of a native woman and hence he got rid of Amy, an Indian Ayah, early on. Or the same can be said when William was not allowed to have much to do with Moti Lal, an Indian secretary who taught him Hindustani. He was also not allowed to mix with an Indian clerk and a chaprassi (peon). All this points to Scott's image of the Indians as inferior people.

Afterwards William's father was appointed the Political Agent to the Tradura Agency. Apart from Tradura there were five neighbouring principalities in the Agency: Jundapur, Shakura, Premkar, Trassura and Durhat. As he started growing, Mrs Canterbury, William's governess, taught him how the British were qualified to rule the Indians. She said:

> "Men like your father have put down all the feudal injustices."
> "Men like your father have given them standards". "By leaving them with the crowns and palaces they had when we first conquered India men like your father have shown them that the English understand true value".[10]

This type of teaching clearly brings to our notice how the image of British as superior was consciously built up in India. Due to this they considered themselves to be the only people fit to rule the country, the feeling that made them abuse the Indian national struggle for Independence. This is to be seen when Grayson Hume, William's tutor, for example, talks about Indian leaders like Gandhi as leaders who would rather 'starve than fight'.[11] That the British considered Indians unfit for running a democratic government is clear from the following lines:

> There was so much we had to teach the Indians before they could rule themselves. That was what Father's job was about, although the princes were a different problem. We had two jobs in India. The Princes knew how to rule but we had to teach them democracy. The Indians of British India knew about democracy but had to be taught how to rule.[12]

This brings to our notice the superior image of the British in India. Occasionally, Scott makes a beautiful use of pictures and paintings in his recreation of the past. For example, in one of the pictures of the Battle of Plassey, with Clive brandishing a sword and flies fluttering in the breeze, shows how the British rule in India began and how the British like Conways were proud of having such pictures in their houses. Their belief in their superiority can be seen when William says that 'his father stared at him with the face of a boy to whom an Indian career was a living death, a cold and bitter duty he would support only because the genes had made him prone to the call of duty and had shaped him to endure cold.[13] So, the fact that in spite of the adverse conditions in India they were strongly committed to their moral duty in India speaks of their belief in racial superiority of the British.

According to Prescott, the historical imagination of the novelist involves the use of documentary sources like letters, books, journals, etc.[14] This can be illustrated with reference to Scott's art of historical novel as well. He makes his protagonist scour the political history shelves of the public library and consider the following books so as to throw light on the British Indian history: *India Since Partition; Betrayal in Delhi; The New Dominion; The Last Viceroy; Farewell to Princes; The Integration of the Indian States* and titles like that.[15] Making use of these sources William throws light on various aspects of British Indian history, particularly the history of the Indian princes. For example,

Scott has stated how after the departure of the British the princes were rendered powerless. The resultant sense of loss of identity of the princes becomes clear when Ranjit Rao's son says:

> We all became bannias, old man, adding figures, squabbling about knives and forks.[16]

At the time of Independence one of the most important issues was that of the future of the princes. In this connection it is to be noted that the princes stood by the British and attacked the leaders of Indian National Congress, the fact that can be found realistically depicted by Scott. For instance, the princes' belief in the British is to be seen when the author thinks of Dingy Row's eldest son in the following manner:

> He had a high opinion of the then Viceroy, Wavell, who, he knew, would "sort out these chaps Nehru and Jinnah", and wouldn't "sell the states down the river".[17]

The Princes' distrust in the democratic attitude of the Congress and belief in the British paramountcy is further seen when Dingy Row's son states:

> "We've stood by the Crown," Dingy Row's son said, "and the Crown'll stand by us. The jackals aren't going to feed on us. Wavell will see to it. So shall we. So will men like your father."[18]

By jackals he meant the Indian politicians of British India whom he described as 'at each other's bloody throats, carving up the country and getting rid of the princes if they get the chance'.

Or their belief in the treaty with the British and distrust in the intellectual inability of the national leaders to run the democratic government is reflected in the following lines:

> Sometimes he talked about Gopalkand's age-old treaty with Britain, the paramount power,..., one that would protect Gopalkand through thick and thin, leave her free, independent and benevolently autocratic if British India become free and

Independent and what he called a subdemocracy of pseudo-intellectuals, fat bannias and religious maniacs.[19]

Thus, Scott depicts the British as superior rulers to that of the Indians which is a recurrent point of reference throughout his novels.

Scott has quite realistically described the decline and fall of the Indian princes while maintaining the historical factuality as far as the persons, dates and events are concerned, the fact that brings in Nield's view that 'a novel is rendered historical by the introduction of dates, personages or events to which identification can be really given.[20] For instance, Scott is quite factual in stating that the British Cabinet Mission had to explain that Independence for British India would mean the end of paramountcy, the end of treaties the British no longer had the means to adhere.[21] And thus the disillusionment of the princes is recorded which is also historically quite true. Or the total downfall of the princes in the post-Independence India is noted by him in the following manner:

> The maharajas ate crow. With nearly six hundred of them they ate it in different ways, a few eagerly, most reluctantly, some by forcible feeding. Some threatened to accede to Pakistan even if geographically such an accession would have been nonsensical; others were as much coerced into accession by their own people as diplomatically persuaded by the politicians of the new India.[22]

In these lines Scott has described the plight of the Indian princes and their reluctance to merge with the free India which is historically quite factual.

The next important aspect regarding the British Indian history that Scott depicts is the effect of the partition on India and the relationship between the states and the Congress. That the rift between the Hindus and the Muslims accompanied by the partition resulted into the mass killing is quite convincingly recorded by Scott in these words:

> During the massacres that accompanied the partition they'd seen the trains coming into Lahore piled with bodies of people who'd been killed between there and Delhi, either Muslims killed by Hindus or Hindus killed by Muslims, never British; the British were treated with great courtesy.[23]

Here Scott points out the savagery in the Indians which was at the base of the communal riots; at the same time he points out how superior the British were since he believes in spite of the turbulent nature of the situation they were not killed, on the contrary, they were respected.

In this context he also maintains that the communal riots were created by the Congress for their own interest, the fact that shows how Scott denies to approve of the efforts made by the Congress in the direction of the self-rule for India. He writes:

> They had riots in their own capitals, riots they described as raised by Congress-inspired rabble but which Congress described as the struggle of their enslaved subjects for democratic freedom.[24]

The princes became critical of the Congress because it was the Congress who took over from the British. The transfer of power was considered by the princes as a tragic affair. Their strong feelings about the Congress are to be seen when Scott writes about Dingy Row's son:

> The whole thing had been an awful bore. A tragedy too, not that he personally had anything to lose except a deficit in the annual budget. But the English had thrown the states to the wolves, hadn't they?[25]

The brutal treatment given to the Indians can be noticed when they are described as 'wolves' by Scott.

The relationship between the princes and the British is also highlighted. In this respect it is interesting to note how Scott has recreated the life of the British in India, particularly the privileged treatment they received from the Indian princes and how their consciousness of the rulers' superiority is reflected through this recreation. First of all it is significant to know how Scott has shown the decadence of the princes, the thing which renders them unable to run the state. For example, if we minutely examine his description of the state of Tradura we come to know how they were decaying. He describes the state of affairs in the following manner:

> Ranjit Raosingh's succession was assured. He had sons, five I think it was. The eldest by his first wife, the Maharani, was

a man of middle-age. There were grandsons and daughters. There was a second official wife and there were two concubines, one of them a Goanese half-caste who had been beautiful.[26]

The decadence is further noted by Scott when he describes an incident of succession to the 'gaddi'. During his father's term of office Ranjit Raosingh was preoccupied with the belief that his eldest son intended to enforce his abdication on the grounds of age and health. This was the excuse, anyway, that he put forward to justify his wish to nominate as heir his son by the Goanese half-caste. There was once a poison scare. The Goanese was seized with violent abdominal pains after a meal. In this respect Ranjit Rao suspected the Maharani of trying to get rid of the concubine who was turning him against his true son. Apart from the problem of succession Scott is also interested in pointing out the feudal attitude towards women in the states. He writes about the Maharaja's women:

He kept his women in palace purdah. Grayson-Hume, discussing Hindu customs, told me that on the few occasions Father met the Maharani she and her women talked to him from behind a screen.[27]

To be brief, Scott's overall impression of the state is expressed when he says that 'there was feudal poverty, inefficiency and corruption among officials in the state.'[28] Against this background he points out the role of the British in the states. Scott's belief in the Britishers' strong sense of reforming the things is clearly reflected in the faith William had in his father's ability 'to curb tendencies in the direction of poverty, corruption, etc., with his sound advice and shining example, and the power he subtly wielded as the representative of the British Crown'.[29] Thus, in showing the inferiority of the Indians he means the superiority of the British.

The next important aspect of the British Indian history that Scott has depicted is the treatment given to the British by the Japanese in the war and the formation of Indian National Army in Japan. William joined the West country territorial regiment in England in 1939 and later was commissioned. They defended beaches at home from 1939 until they went to Malaya where in Pig Eye Camp he was imprisoned by the Japanese for three and a half years. William records how they were treated by the Japanese there. For instance, the following account of the treatment given to his men is sufficient enough to point out the inhuman element in it:

> My men were roped together by their wrists and ankles. They were being made to hobble round in a circle. The Japanese were pricking them with bayonets.... The youngest, a fair, good-looking man called Bracegirdle, was out away from his companions, stripped, held by the shoulders and ankles and sexually assaulted three times. After each man had finished with him he was jerked upright, twisted round and made to look at the man whose turn was coming next. When there seemed to be no more comers they let him go.[30]

The intention of the author behind colouring the image of the Japanese as inhumans is to criticise the members of the Indian National Army who joined the Japanese. Scott appears realistic when he writes how the INA in Pig Eye in Japan came into being:

> The camp was divided into three: Indians, British, sick-bay compound. After a while a lot of the Indians were suborned and formed themselves into a unit of what was called the Indian National Army, which was inspired by Subhas Chandra Bose.[31]

What is interesting in his account of the INA is Scott's views regarding the Indians. He points out how in the INA the Indians were not sympathetic towards their own people. Those Indians who refused to join the INA unit were sent away, but some of them came to the sick-bay to be treated for injuries, mostly for burns from being held over a fire, or ruptures, or internal lacerations caused by sharpened bamboo stakes. In this respect he expresses his views about Indians. For example, he narrates the story of Rajput Subedar:

> At first we thought the Japanese had tortured them but a Rajput Subedar said his chief torturer was his own Havildar-Major who had assumed the INA rank of Lieutenant. He said his orderly also suffered, had been beaten to death with leather belts.[32]

Thus, the image of Indians as depicted in the context of the INA is that of the inferior people which is quite recurrent in Scott's novels.

The consideration of the symbol of the birds of paradise used by Scott in this novel gets the historical meaning which contributes to the historical imagination of the author. The symbol is presented in the context of the discussion of the British Indian history against the background of the present. And it is one of the significant aspects of the historical novel, as in the opinion of Fleishman, 'the historical novelist writes transtemporally: he is rooted in the history of his own time and yet can conceive another and in ranging back into history he discovers not merely his own origins but his historicity, his existence as a historical being'.[33] The symbol is central to the novel which is pointed out by C.W. Mann when he says that 'the Birds of Paradise of the title hung stuffed in a great cage on a Maharaja's estate, and the writer's childhood impression of their beauty and inaccessibility is a haunting image which recurs again and again'.[34] Patrick Swinden believes that there has been an explicit identification of the birds as symbols of the raj, and the Princely states during the British occupation of India.[35] Or, according to Martin Levin, the stuffed birds of paradise that inhabit the cage are harbingers of futility, 'Omens of all the marvellous things that were going to happen later - but didn't.[36] The symbol is probably better explained by the author himself in the following words of Krishi:

> Well, then, Krishi said, the family joke was that the birds in the cage were thought to be like the British Raj, creatures who took it for granted they excited wonder and admiration wherever they went and had no idea that they were dead from the neck up and the neck down, weren't flying at all and were imprisoned in their own conceit way... Krishi said that the family joke had misfired, though, because history had shown that it was the princes of India who were dead, in spite of all their finery and high flown postures. The British had stuffed them and burnished their fine featuers, but as princes they were dead even if they weren't dead as men, and if not actually dead then anyway buried alive in a cage the British had never attempted really to open.[37]

Thus, the symbol that carries the historic meaning helps us understand the decadence of Indian princes. No doubt, it points out the superior image of the British in the Raj.

The British Raj is compared with the present day India which, the author believes, is still backward. The Indians have failed to achieve success after Independence. He describes the post-Independence India as a land 'full of fragile people clothed in cotton and moving sedately to their own mournful music'.[38] This backwardness of India and superiority of the British is further noted in the following words:

> It seems sad, that on the one hand such exquisite creatures should leave out their lives and exhibit their charms only in these wild inhospitable regions, doomed for ages yet to come to hopeless barbarism; while on the other hand, should civilized man ever reach these distant lands, and bring moral, intellectual and physical light into the recesses of these virgin forests.[39]

Thus, in the recreation of the past there is an inevitable relationship between the past and the present which becomes a highly significant point in establishing the author's point of view; and we can understand why Swinden says that the recognition of how the truth of the past fades and reshapes itself in the interests of the present is at the heart of Scott's novel.[40] To be precise, Scott believes that India has not developed since Independence; it is not the world for which the Raj prepared India in' which she struggles to survive. In a way, he points out the superiority of the British Raj.

NOTES AND REFERENCES

1   Paul Scott, "The Raj", Frank Moraes & Edward Howe (ed.) *India* (Delhi: Vikas, 1974), p. 88.

2   Patrick Swinden, *Paul Scott; Images of India* (London: Macmillan, 1980), p. 47.

3   Paul Scott, "India: A Post-Forsterian View,¹ Mary Stocks (ed.), *Essays By Divers Hands* (London: OUP, 1970), Vol. XXXVI, p. 120.

4   Paul Scott, *The Birds of Paradise* (London: Heinemann, 1962), p. 251.

5   H. Butterfield, *The Historical Novel* (Cambridge; Univ. Press, 1924), p. 106.

6   Charles Allen, *Raj; A Scrapbook of British India* (1877- 1947) (Harmondsworth: Penguin, 1979), p. 93.

7   Manohar Malgonkar, "Princely India," Frank Moraes and Edward Howe (ed.) *India* (Delhi; Vikas, 197 4), p. 92,

8   Avrom Fleishman, *The English Historical Novel; Walter Scott to Virginia Woolf* (Baltimore & London: Johns Hopkins Press, 1971), p. lo.

9   Orville Prescott, *In My Opinion: An Inguiry into the Contemporary Novel* (New York: Charter Books, 1963), p. 134.

10 Paul Scott, *The Birds of Paradise* (London: Heinemann, 1962), p. 32.

11 *Ibid.,* p. 35.

12 *Ibid.,* p. 36.

13 *Ibid.,* p. 113.

14 Orville Prescott, *The Undying Past* (New York: Doubleday & Co. inc., 1961), p. 17.

15 Paul Scott, *The Birds of Paradise* (London: Heinemann, 1962), p. 196.

16 *Ibid.,* p. 230.

17 *Ibid.,* p. 151.

18 *Ibid.*

19 *Ibid.*

20 Jonathan Nield, *A Guide to the Best Historical Novels and Tales* (New York: Burt Franklin, Rpt., 1968), p. XVIII.

21 Paul Scott, *The Birds of Paradise* ('London: Heinemann, 1962), p. 153.

22 *Ibid.,* pp. 197-98.

23 *Ibid.,* p.234.

24 *Ibid.,* p. 198.

25 *Ibid.*, p. 230.

26 *Ibid.*, p. 45.

27 *Ibid.*, pp. 46-47.

28 *Ibid,* p. 45.

29 *Ibid.*

30 *Ibid.*, pp. 155-56.

31 *Ibid.*, p. 158.

32 *Ibid.*, p. 158.

33 Avrom Fleishman, *The English Historical Novel; Walter Scott to Virginia Woolf* (Baltimore & London: Johns Hopkins Press, 1971), p. 5.

34 C.W. Mann, rev. of *The Birds of Paradise* by Paul Scott, <u>Library Journal</u>, Vol. 87, No. 14, Aug. 1962, p. 2778.

35 Patrick Swinden, *Paul Scott; Images of India* (London: Macmillan, 1980), p. 55.

36 Martin Levin, rev. of *The Birds of Paradise* by Paul Scott, *The New York Times Book Review,* Sept. 30, 1962, p. 44.

37 Paul Scott, *The Birds of Paradise* (London: Heinemann, 1962), p. 243.

38 *Ibid.,* p. 174.

39 *Ibid.,,* p. 263.

40 Patrick Swinden, *Paul Scott; Images of India* (London: Macmillan, 1980), p. 47.

CHAPTER IV

The *Raj Quartet*

1. *The Jewel in the Crown*

The Jewel in the Crown (1966)

The fact that Paul Scott defies the tendency of most of his critics to compare *The Jewel in the Crown* (1966) with E.M. Forster's *A Passage to India* (1924) only because both the novels handle similar theme - the rape of an English girl by an Indian causing racial hostilities - raises one of the crucial questions facing the readers of <u>The Jewel</u>: what constitutes Scott's defiance?[1] Scott himself comes forward to answer this question, which is quite explicitly stated by him at the beginning of his paper read at the Royal Society of Literature on 5th December, 1968. He states:

> The Anglo-India I took my own passage to was not quite the same as the one Forster knew and brilliantly recorded. The differences were marginal, but they existed. The rate of history's flow is pretty slow, but in twenty years it can advance a yard or two, and did, even in Anglo-India. It is a third or quarter of the average man's life.[2]

Scott's observation sounds true because though *A Passage to India* was published in 1924 it was started and mostly written during Forster's 1912-13 visit, which means that historically its framework is that of India before the First World War. The situation in India had undergone a great change since then. The Indian National Congress was no longer limited to an intellectual coterie; the independence movement had taken hold of the imagination of all Indians down to the toiling peasantry. Gandhi had launched his Civil Disobedience movement in 1920, and things were no longer non-violent after the 1919 massacre of peaceful Indians by General Dyer at Jallianwallah Bagh in Amritsar. At this moment we must note that unlike Forster, Scott gives much importance to the historical developments and admits that 'it would not be awfully wise to write about Anglo-India discounting the actual, progress of history[3]. And we, therefore, in conformity with Paul Gray, admit that 'all of the past comparisons to E.M. Forster should by now be declared totally irrelevant to Scott, though, perhaps inevitable whenever an English novelist takes on India[4] So, the problem before us remains: how does Scott reveal his idea of progress in history through the novel? Scott's sympathetic consideration of the things which are essentially English and denouncement of essentially Indian things constitute his idea of progress.

The reader's immersion in the turbulent period of Indian history begins when he is asked to imagine a flat landscape where the ochre walls of the houses in the old town are seen - the walls that are stained with their bloody past and uneasy present. The importance that Scott attributes to the historical events in the novel is quite obvious in the following lines:

> In 1942, which was the year the Japanese defeated the British army in Burma and Mr. Gandhi began preaching sedition in India, the English then living in the civil and military cantonment of Mayapore had to admit that the future did not look propitious. They had faced bad times before, though, and felt what they could face them again, that now they knew where they stood and there could be no more heart searching for quite a while yet about the rights and wrongs of their colonial-imperialist policy and administration.[5]

Scott is quite true to facts which speak of his historical accuracy. However, it is to be noted that he does not merely attempt to write historical fiction by using material from history but that he recreates it through the artistic mode of his own, and in doing so he exemplifies Butterfield's idea of the historical novel:

> In order to catch things in the life of the past, and to make a bygone age live again, history must not merely be extended by inventing episodes; it must be turned into a novel; it must be 'put to fiction' as a poem is put to music.[6]

So, in the context of the fusion of the fact and fiction it is significant to note that apart from an interesting plot, Scott's historical imagination makes use of various images, symbols, characters and interesting dialogues which unfold the complicated nature of human beings. The fact that Scott narrates the history in human terms that reveal the complex human relationship between the people and the places becomes quite clear when he says:

> This is a story of a rape, of the events that led upto it and followed it and of the place in which it happened. There are the action, the people and the place.[7]

The quotation clearly indicates that Scott is very much conscious of the unity of places and people and circumstances that exist together and it is significant because in the deeper movement of history they appear to coalesce. The point of human relations is quite seriously considered by Scott in his entire creative activity. Since the colonial world is characterized by domination and exploitation, according to Fanon, and in the imposition of a foreign culture and civilization, according to Said, the racial discrimination mediated by all the institutions of colonial society determine the individual and social conduct of the colonized person both in his living together with the other colonized and in his relations with the colonist. In this respect, the question of human relations becomes of paramount importance when he says:

> .... the affair that began on the evening of August 9th, 1942 in Mayapore, ended with spectacle of two nations in violent opposition, not for the first time, nor as yet for the last because they were then still locked in an imperial embrace of such long standing and subtlety it was no longer possible for them to know whether they hated or loved one another.[8]

Thus, Scott's conception of historical reality was deeply influenced by his imagining it immersed in the flow of time. It gave him a feeling for the unity of all the many people and places and circumstances that exist together in time; to a superficial eye they may appear separate and unrelated except by chance, but in the deeper movement of history they appear to coalesce.

The Jewel in the Crown is concerned with two main events in the civil commotion - the commotion that involved an attack on a European woman, Miss Edwina Crane, the Supervisor of Protestant Schools in Mayapore District followed by the murder of her Indian colleague, Mr D.R. Chaudhuri and the rape of an English girl, Miss Daphne Manners, by a gang of hooligans in the area known as the Bibighar Gardens. These two incidents are narrated as the portents of the great danger to the English people and it made them to conclude that the safety of English people, particularly of their women, was in grave peril. These incidents, no doubt, are fictitious in nature; but by setting them against the background of one of the most important historic events - the All India Congress voting in favour of Gandhi's Civil Disobedience Resolution on 8th August 1942, a resolution under which the British had been called upon to leave India and Mahatma Gandhi and the entire working committee were arrested that followed the civil violence all over the country - Scott has imbued them with historical authenticity. Substantiating Scott's serious concern with history Martin Levin states that besides story-telling, Mr. Scott also used his remarkable technique to portray a place and time, a society and its social arrangements, that are now history.[9] Here Scott highlights three aspects of British Indian history, viz., the colonial structure of Indian society that provides two distinct images of Anglo-Indian and native ways of life, the Indian nationalist freedom struggle and the Partition of India which was accompanied by the communal discord between Hindus and Muslims. Within this point of reference I would discuss the technique through which Scott has recreated the British Indian history with the help of various images, symbols, a deep thematic structure and some remarkable characters.

As we go through the novel it seems that his idea of progress governs his aesthetic recreation of the Raj which consists of the contrasting images of Britishers and Indians. The very technique of contrast unfolds his progressive outlook on the part of the British. The first is the image of India and the Indians. The most important image of India that emerges in the novel is that India is a muddle, the image that conforms to the images created by Kipling and Forster. For example, the image of death and decay is recreated by him in the third part of the novel where we notice Sister Ludmila, a lady, who, in those days, used to run a sanctuary and on every Wednesday morning used to set out on foot from the cluster of old buildings where she fed the hungry, ministered to the sick, and cleansed and comforted those who for want of her nightly scavanging would have died in the street. The intensity of this problem can be found in her observation about India when she says:

> India is a place where men died, still die, in the open, for
> want of succour, for want of shelter, for want of respect for
> the dignity of death.[10]

Contributory to this image are the images of dirt, insanity and loneliness. For example, in one of his letters to Colin Lindsey Hari mentions that "in India everybody shouts. There'll be a pedlar or a beggar at the gate out front. And he'll be shouting." He also writes about India's love for insanity when he refers to a man who screams. When he first heard him he thought he was a madman who'd got lose. But he was a madman who had never been locked up because he was treated as a holy man. In this way, the Indians are ridiculed in the following manner:

> His madness is thought of as a sign that God has personally noticed him. He is, therefore, holier than any of the so-called sane people. Perhaps underneath this idea that he's holy is the other idea that insane is the only sensible thing for an Indian to be, and what they all wish they were.[11]

Again, the image of Pandit Baba Sahib who used to teach Hindi to Hari also highlights the Indians' indecency and unpunctuality. Hari's description of Pandit Baba is quite eloquent:

> The pandit has a dirty turban and a grey beard. He smells of garlic. It sickens me to catch his breath. The lessons are a farce because he speaks no English I recognise. Sometimes he doesn't turn up at all, or turns up an hour late. They have no conception of time. To me they are still 'they.'[12]

Mr. Robin White's image of India, which is no other than that of dirt and smell, also contributes to the above-cited views. He describes India as follows:

> But I hated India - the real India behind the pipe-puffing myth. I hated the loneliness, and the dirt, the smell, the conscious air of superiority that one couldn't get through the day without putting on like a sort of protective purdah. I hated Indians because they were the most immediately available target and couldn't hit back except in subtle ways that made me hate them even more.'[13]

This recurrence of the images of India is significant as it helps draw inference about Scott's attitude towards India. A close look at the image of India as depicted by Scott brings to our notice that he uses the same conventional image of India as depicted by Kipling or Forster. Though, unlike Scott, Kipling takes the magic of India, its dark secrets, mystery, romantic splendours as his major interests, there is a sort of similarity between them when he describes India in several of his poems, short stories and the novels like *Kim*. For example, his famous poem, 'The White Man's Burden', presents the image of the Indian as a 'half devil and half child'. Similarly Forster's vision of India is essentially a vision of chaos when he admits with dismay: 'Little is clear-cut in India'.[14] Or, the most important image of India that emerges in *A Passage to India* is a muddle, which becomes evident when Fielding goes on to say, "A mystery is only a highsounding term for a muddle, Aziz and I know that India's a muddle.[15]

Thus, in the same manner, Scott's creation of the image of India reveals his vision. The fact that Scott always focuses on India as a quintessence of evil is a clue to the idea of progress that was a governing principle in his novels. He seems to subscribe Kipling's idea of 'a white man's burden'. This can be illustrated by referring to a few more images created by him. The image of a native town visited by Miss Crane can be cited as a good example. She describes it as follows:

> .... the native town which she had entered on one occasion to inspect a Hindu temple which had frightened her with its narrow dirty streets, its disgusting poverty, its raucous dissonant music, its. verminous dogs, its starving,-mutilated beggars, its fat white sacred Brahmini bulls and its ragged populations of men and women who looked so resentful in comparison with the servants and other officiating natives of the cantonment.[16]

Thus, if we think in the line of Fanon, Scott being a colonizer paints the native town as a place of ill fame, a world without spaciousness which is starved of bread, meat and light. Scott explores this pattern of a native town when he describes the town of Mayapore with an added dimension of the description of its divisions. He writes:

> The church was situated not far from Miss Crane's bungalow, close to the Mandir Gate bridge, one of the two bridges that spanned the river-bed that divided the civil lines from the native town.... On the native town side of the Mandir Gate bridge was to be found the Tirupati temple.... Between the Mandir Gate bridge, on the civil lines side, and the second bridge, the Bibighar bridge, lived the Eurasian community,

close at hand to the depots, godowns and offices of the railway station. The railway followed the course of the river-bed. The tracks crossed the roads that led to the bridges. At the bridgeheads on the civil lines side, consequently, there were level crossings whose gates, when closed to let railway traffic through, sealed both bridges off, making a barrier between the European and native population.[17]

The detailed description of the town makes an explicit statement on the typical colonial structure of the town which unfolds how the European and native populations maintained their separate identities by living in exclusively separate areas of the town. That this structure is representative can be proved by pointing out some other places in Anglo-Indian fiction. In *A Passage to India*, for example, Forster brings home the division between the British rulers and native subjects by the physical separation of the low-lying, squalid and haphazardly built Indian section of Chandrapore from the clean and orderly civil station on the rise where the Europeans lived. The character of the two communities is skilfully suggested in the topography and structure of their respective residential areas which have nothing in common - the civil station 'shares nothing with the city except the overarching sky.' [18] As opposed to the Indian section, the civil station is 'sensibly planned' with a 'red-brick club on its brow' and bungalows disposed along 'roads that intersect at right angles' - these roads, named after victorious British generals, are "symbolic of the net Great Britain had thrown over India.[19] Thus, taking the representative structure of Mayapore into account, John Mellors has rightly pointed out that 'Mayapore is a fictitious place, but it could be anyone of a number of medium to large cities in the U.P., each with its cantonment separated topographically, architecturally and culturally from the densely populated Indian town'.[20] The image of a native town is not devoid of a Protestant Church in India - the institution that symbolises the Britishers' imperial service in India. The church is described as follows:

When Miss Crane came to the Church she turned into the compound and went up the broad gravel path, past the hummocky grave marked by the headstones of those who had died far from home, but who in their resting place, had they woken, might have been comforted by the English look of the Church and its yard and the green trees planted there.[21]

The very phrase 'the English look' in this description suggests Scott's conscious effort to point out the Britishers' pride in their identity as British.

Other equally significant components of Scott's image of India are the Indian education system, Indian social structure and the plight of women in Indian society. So far as the education in India is concerned Scott believes that because the Indians were lacking in education it was the mission of the British people to educate the Indians. This point is illustrated in the meeting between Mr Grant and Miss Crane when Grant says:

> "There are of course a great number of schools throughout the
> country, of various denominations, all committed to educating
> what I suppose we must call the heathen".[22]

The word 'heathen' used by Grant points out that the British considered Indians as backward people who needed education. It also registers Scott's idea of progress in history. At the root of this educating mission, naturally, there lies, according to Scott, the unacademic atmosphere in India which is clearly evidenced in the following description given by Grant of an Indian school:

> "... The school here, for instance. A handful of children at the
> best of times. At the times of the festivals none. I mean, of
> course, the Hindu and Moslem festivals. The children come,
> you see, mainly for the chappattis, and in the last riots the
> school was set fire too.....".[23]

Here, it is to be noted that Scott does not distinguish between Hindus and Moslems. He treats them just as Indians. Contributory to the image of school is the image of an Indian teacher. Here, the involvement of Mr Narayan, one of the mission school teachers, in unacademic activities becomes the point of Scott's criticism. The image of a teacher is conveyed to us when Mr Narayan is described as 'a man who was suspected of selling contraceptives to Christian and progressive Hindu families, who himself had an ever-pregnant wife, and a large, noisy, undisciplined family of boys and girls'.[24] In this way, the image of an Indian academic institution forms the part of the overall image of India as a place of disrepute.

The next important point of reference is the depiction of Indian social structure which throws light on the caste-system in India, the position of women and orthodoxy of Indians. He refers to the rigid caste-system in India. His depiction of the feelings of Edwina Crane when she goes to dine with Mr Chaudhuri, an assistant teacher in the mission school, throws light on the fact that the untouchables were not accepted by the other castes as their equals, Scott, through Edwina's feelings, points out the position of the untouchables in India in the following lines:

> A woman servant waited on them, the same woman who did the cooking. Miss Crane would have felt more comfortable if the woman had been an untouchable because that would have proved, in the Chaudhuries, emancipation from the rigidity of caste. But the woman was a Brahmin.[25]

The problem of untouchability was so serious in the pre-Independence India that it reminds us one of the prominent Indo-Anglian novelists, Mulk Raj Anand, who, especially in his *Untouchable* (1933), condemns untouchability as a crime against human dignity and points out the evils in Indian society which he considers perverted and decadent. However, he presents it from the viewpoint of the Marxian philosophy which is altogether different from the viewpoint of Scott who presents it as a colonizer.

Scott subtly comments on the hidebound orthodox Indian family in the fifth part of the novel, 'Young Kumar', which depicts the picture of Indian middle-class society. The story begins with Dulip Kumar, Hari's father. The Kumars, the landowners in a district of the United Provinces, were rich by Indian standards and loyal to the crown. The whole story of Dulip Kumar, his education and marriage, aims at the criticism of orthodox nature of the Indians.[26] For example, Dulip's family which consisted of seven children was regarded auspicious, the fact that shows the blind belief of the Indians. Their attitude towards education is also to be noted when he tells that of the four brothers only Dulip went to the Government College since his family thought that to study at the college was a waste of time. Or their dislike for education is further illustrated when he says that when he went to attend the college, a hundred miles away from his place, his elder sisters and sisters-in-law looked at him as if he were setting out on some shameful errand. Their belief in the horoscope is shown strong when, at the time of his marriage, the Kumars found out a girl whose horoscope, according to the astrologers, was in an auspicious confluence with his own. Again at the time of fixing the date of wedding the advice of the astrologers was sought. The money-minded nature of such families is also revealed when Dulip opposed the idea of early marriage since he wanted to go to England for his further studies. But more than education what was important for his father was the money that would come by the way of dowry. His father, therefore, says to him:

> What you call your career has not yet begun. Perhaps you have overlooked the advantage of the dowry your wife would bring to this household?[27]

Thus, the entire story of Dulip Kumar is a satire upon the orthodox Indian society of which especially patriarchal aspect of the family is exposed by Scott.

The discussion of the orthodox Indian family brings in a major issue, i.e., the plight of women in such a family. Here it is seen that the image of Indian woman depicted by Scott is no more than a caricature. For example, in her criticism of Mrs Chaudhuri, Miss Crane thought that 'she was uninstructed in the ways of the sophisticated world and had a remarkably old fashioned notion of the role of a wife'.[28] Again the image of Indian woman and her aloofness is created when he describes the relationship between an Indian husband and his wife. For instance, at the time of parties, they didn't come very close to each other. The British were very critical of the Indian habit of keeping men and women so well separated that a mixed party was almost more than an English host and hostess could bear to visualize. This relationship is further exposed in the following words:

> The English always assumed that Indian women found it distasteful to be publicly in mixed company and so there was a tacit understanding that a married Indian officer would appear even less frequently than his bachelor colleagues because he professed to stay in quarters with his wife.[29]

The backwardness of Indian women in education is also described by Scott when he tells the story of how the parents of Kamala, Dulip's wife, would not let her go to school. Dulip, however, tried to get hold of a teacher from the Zenana Mission, an organization that set teachers into orthodox Indian homes to instruct-the women privately, but the Mission lost interest when it was learnt that only one young girl would attend the lessons.[30] The consideration of Scott's image of Indian woman poses a question: has Scott depicted a realistic image of Indian woman? The answer can be sought by comparing Scott with a few of the Indo-Anglian novelists who have also penned the image of Indian woman. In Nayantara Sahgal's *This Time of Morning,* for instance, a woman is shown struggling against custom. She knows well that she has been betrothed to Vijay without her consent and she resents this, for she feels that she has been acquired as a business transaction, rather than for what she is, a woman yearning for love. Or in her novel, *The Nature of Passion,* Mrs Ruth Prawer Jhabwala depicts Kanta, a young woman who, regardless of Hindu marriage traditions, not only marries outside her caste, but consents to marry Chandra of her own free will. Thus, the image of woman as depicted by Sahagal or Jhabwala is assertive and highly individualistic which is the reverse of Scott's, the fact that speaks of Scott's narrow understanding of Indian woman. In this respect, then, it won't be an exaggeration if it is said that Scott also becomes one of the Anglo-Indian writers whose narrow vision prevented him from doing full justice to the image of Indian woman. Meena Shirwadkar has rightly pointed out the logic behind it. In her opinion, these writers were conditioned by the biased relationship of the ruling race with that of the ruled. Or, they did not know the languages of India well; nor did they see the Indian woman at close quarters, for there were many rigid customs that did not allow an outsider to have closer glimpses of the Indian woman hidden in her home or behind the purdah. The few Indian women they came to know were either the rich, the westernised and the christianised women or the servant-women, the ayahs and the native women taken up as mistresses.[31]

The image of Indian princes also forms a major part of Scott's recreation of British Indian history because it also talks about his progressive attitude towards history. The idea of progress does not involve the mere fact of change, a change is progressive only if it is felt to represent certain values. By depicting the decadent life of the princes Scott derogates them and in doing so ascribes the validity of moral values to the Britishers and in this sense presents the idea of progress. Scott does not fully develop the image of the Indian prince in *The Jewel in the Crown* as he does in one of his earlier novels, *The Birds of Paradise.* At the very beginning of the second part of the novel Scott tells us the history of the Bibighar and the MacGregor House where Daphne was staying with Lili Chatterjee, an Indian friend of her aunt's. The reference to this place becomes important as it shows the decadent life of Indian princes.

The original building where the MacGregor House now stands was created in the late 18th century by an Indian prince who conceived a deep passion for a singer. The house stands in the middle of the garden. When the singer died the prince grieved and died of a broken heart. The house was deserted and closed. The prince's son who succeeded to the 'gaddi' despised his father for his futile attachment to the singer. He built another house nearby, the Bibighar, where he kept his courtesans. Due to his voluptuousness he was deposed, imprisoned and his state was annexed. The decayed house of the singer was rebuilt by a red-faced Scottish Nabob called MacGregor who feared God and favoured Muslims, and was afraid of temples. The story goes that he burnt the Bibighar to the ground because he said it had been an abomination. He died at the hands of mutinous sepoys.[32] The history of these places vividly conveys the character of Indian princes, particularly their self-indulgent way of life and the negligence of their duties which presents just the opposite of the British character. Though depicted from purely British point of view, Scott's image of an Indian prince, to some extent, conforms to the image created by Mulk Raj Anand in *The Private Life of an Indian Prince* (1953). Anand gives a picture of an extravagent, debauched and voluptuous prince. However, in pointing out these similarities we must remember that Scott shows his interest in pointing out how the British were superior rulers to the Indian ones. Anand, with his proletarian ideals, makes the prince an object of hatred and a butt of ridicule.

To point out the full significance of these places - the Bibighar and the MacGregor House - as symbols, as portrayed by Benita Parry and Patrick Swinden, is to show clearly the power of Scott's historical imagination. One of the characteristic features of Scott's fiction is the relationships between the people and the places where they meet. In the present novel the event of the rape of Daphne Manners is related to the places that have a symbolic relation to each other, and whose symbolic ambiance is brought out by the author in a vivid description of their histories. Thus, as pointed out by Benita Parry, the history of these places symbolises the connections and separations between whites and blacks.[33] The symbol is further illustrated by Swinden in the following lines:

> The history suggests that the MacGregor House and the
> Bibighar Gardens are closely connected by the passions of
> those who have inhabited them in the past. But it also suggests

that the connection has always issued in violence, and, finally, separation especially when the lovers have tried to cross the seemingly impregnable barrier of race.[34]

Thus, it is through the excellent use of symbolic places that Scott recreates the racial exclusiveness of India. So, the images and symbols contribute a lot in recreating the atmosphere of the age which, according to Butterfield, is an inevitable aspect of the historical novel.

Besides the use of places, Scott sometimes makes a beautiful use of paintings and pictures to recreate the past. For example, the recreation of the British colonial history is remarkably done through the description of a picture, much longer in Crane's possession - a semi-historical, semi-allegorical picture entitled "The Jewel in Her Crown." The picture showed "the old Queen surrounded by representative figures of her Indian Empire: princes, landowners, merchants, moneylenders, sepoys, farmers, servants, children, mothers and remarkably clean and tidy beggars. The Queen was sitting on a golden throne, under a crimson canopy, attended by her temporal and spiritual aides: soldiers, statesmen and clergy. The canopied throne was apparently in the open air because there were palm trees and a sky showing a radiant sun bursting out of bulgy clouds such as, in India, heralded the wet monsoon. Above the clouds flew the prayerful figures of the angels who were the benevolent spectators of the scene below. Among the statesmen who stood behind the throne one was painted in the likeness of Mr Disraeli holding up a parchment map of India to which he pointed with obvious pride but tactful humility. An Indian Prince, attended by native servants, was approaching the throne bearing a velvet cushion on which he offered a large jewel and sparkling gem".[35] The historical meaning of the picture is explained by Miss Crane herself. She says to the schoolboys that the gem was simply representative of tribute, and that the jewel of the title was India herself, which had been transferred from the rule of the British India Company to the rule of the British Crown in 1858, the year after the Mutiny.[36] The interpretation points out the development of the British history in India and their strong sense of belonging in the domain of colonial world. Again the interpretation of the same picture given by Mr Cleghorn, an amateur scholar of archeology and anthropology also suggests the idea of British civilizing mission in India. In his opinion, the message in the stylised representation of the tribute was to teach English and at the same time the love of the English. He meant love of their justice, love of their benevolence, love - anyway - of their good intentions.[37] The entire discussion of the picture can be summed up in Parry's words when she says that this allegorical picture is a central and recurrent image in the novel since it is indicative of British paternalism - 'man-bap' - as believed in the British Raj.[38] Parry's views are important because she has pointed out how Scott's subjective values, as pointed out in the introduction, are attributed to the British imperialism in India.

The thoroughly depicted aspect of Anglo-Indian life is an important determinant of British Indian history. One of the most inseparable aspects of the Anglo-Indian life was the club - an institution where the hub of Anglo-Indian social life was to be found and it was, in the words of George Orwell, 'the spiritual citadel, the real seat of the British power, the Nirvana for which native officials and millionaires pine in vain.'[39] For example, Scott describes how the buffet suppers and dances were arranged at various clubs. He also describes how for the duration of the war special arrangements were made to extend club hospitality to as many officers on station as possible. Scott makes use of extensive club-scenes to highlight the British social life in India, particularly, the begotry and racism of the Anglo-Indian society. For example, such a club is described by Daphne Manners in the following manner:

> I never liked the club, but it amuses me - it is so self-conscious about its exclusiveness and yet so vulgar. Someone is always drunk, the talk is mostly scurrilous, and yet its members somehow preserve, goodness knows how, an outward air of rectitude, almost as though there were inviolable 'Rules' for heartless gossip and insufferable behaviour.[40]

This criticism of club-life is further illustrated in the story of the Willingdon Club in Bombay that throws light on the condescending attitude of the British towards the Indians. 'The club was founded by the Viceroy Lord Willingdon in a fit of rage because the Indian guests he invited - in ignorance - to a private banquet at the Royal Yacht Club were turned away from the doors in their Rolls Royces before he cottoned on to what was happening.[41] The exclusiveness of the club can be learnt from a few volumes that mark the stages of the club's administrative history. From the "Members' Book" it is learnt that there were only one or two Indian members of the club. But they were, of course, all officers who held the King Emperor's Commission. It means that the club, by and large, managed to maintain its air of all-white social superiority.

It is obvious that implicit in this discussion is Scott's criticism of the bad side of the Anglo-Indian club life, though it doesn't mean that he is pro-Indians or against the institution of club itself. This observation can be very well established by studying Scott's remarkable use of the technique of contrast. When he describes a club founded by an Indian he always criticises it. For example, when he describes the Mayapore club of which Nello Chatterjee was one of the founder members, he criticises the caste-spirit of the Indians when they named the Club 'Mayapore Hindu Club':

> .... it was always the 'wrong' club. Of course it was originally meant to be an English-type club for Indians who were clubbable, but it was not for nothing that the H for Hindu was suggested. It became a place where the word Hindu was actually more important than the word club. And Hindu did not mean Congress. No. No. Please be aware of the distinction. In this case Hindu meant Hindu Mahasabha. Hindu nationalism - Hindu narrowness.[42]

So, the image of an Indian club is totally in contrast with that of the British club. It also points out the wrong way in which the Indians were anglicised, which, Scott felt, was not a sign of progressive outlook on the part of the Indians. The fact that Scott does not consider the clubs run by Indians significant becomes clear when he makes use of the technique of comparison. He doesn't find one such club important when revisits India after almost twenty five years after the departure of British from India. When he thinks about the extent to which the club has changed since Daphne Manners' days he believes that it would be foolish to suppose that certain contemporary change was a manifestation of anything especially significant, or 'to jump to the conclusion that the obvious preference shown for the room by the handful of English members present proved, in itself, their, subconscious, determination to identify themselves only with what is progressive and therefore, superior.[43] Thus, the club-life throws light on the recreation of the British Indian history.

As pointed out earlier, places and objects play an important role in the historical imagination of Scott since they reveal the relationships between the British and the Indians. One such place, the 'maidan' of Mayapore, attracts our

attention. Again, the technique of comparison is to be noted in the recreation
of this place as well - the comparison made possible by the introduction of an
unknown visitor-narrator who compares the activities during the Raj and after
Independence, The comparative description of the 'maidan' is done from the
viewpoint of showing how once it was sacrosanct to the Civil and Military which
no longer looks now as it did once. The British held their annual gymkhana
and the exhibitions like Flower Show and War Week there. The Indians still
have the gymkhana and flower show there but they are not conducted as the
British used to do. For instance, while describing the present state of affairs he
says that once there was so great a confusion that the club secretary Mr Mitra
offered to resign. Or, as for the cricket, on two occasions in the past five years,
the players walked off in protest at the rowdyism going on among the free-
for-all spectators and once it happened that the spectators invaded the field
in retaliation to protest against the players' highhandedness. There followed
'a pitched battle which the police had to break up with lathi charges just as
they had in the days when the battle going on was of a more serious nature.[44]
This difference between the good old days and the bad present days can also
be found in the comparison of one of the flower shows. For instance, if an
English woman was asked if she went to the flower show last month she would
say, '"Flower Show? why yes - the flower show on the maidan" and would call
nothing forth other than an upward twitch of the eyebrows and a downward
twitch of the mouth, which, after all was voluble enough as an indication that
one had suggested something ridiculous'.[45] It means that since the Indians have
taken over they have made a mess of the entire affair and hence the British
living in Mayapore keep themselves aloof from the things managed in Indian
manner. Implicit here is Scott's opinion that the Independence was responsible
for keeping the Indians away from progress which was the aim of the British in
India. In this way, by relating the present to the past, Scott has shown, in the
words of Mr Pearce, the qualification of a historical novelist that 'however we
look toward the past, we cannot free ourselves from the fact that is somehow
here, now, built into our sense of the past'.

Besides various images Scott is at his best in the character-sketches which
is an important aspect of his historical imagination. As his characters cannot
be separated from the forces of history it can be said that he shows, in the
words of Fleishman, how individual lives were shaped at specific moments
of history, and how this shaping reveals the character of that period.[46] The

juxtaposition of the British and the Indian characters will bring to our notice that the Indian characters play a relatively minor role in *The Jewel in the Crown*. Scott's criticism of Indians can be found in his portrayal of some of the minor characters like Rajendra Singh, the local Sub-Inspector who accompanied Merrick when they visited Sister Ludmila. He is shown as a person who took bribes and stole watches from the men he arrested.[47] Similarly, the Indians are shown as having no sense of maintaining things properly. This becomes clear when Sister Ludmila asks her visitors whether they had visited the Bibighar and the ruins of the house and the garden gone wild in the way most Indians like gardens to be.[48]

Some of the important Indian characters are Lili Chatterjee, repenting on being anglicised, Hari and his father Dulip Kumar, a Brahmin lawyer called Srinivasan and Mr Vidyasagar, a journalist of the *Mayapore Gazette*. It is interesting to note that all these Indian characters are Hindus and they are depicted in the context of Hindu values which are revealed through the institutions like marriage, family, political organisations, etc.

Lili Chatterjee, an anglicised Indian lady, with whom Miss Manners was staying in the MacGregor House, is presented with the problems of a person trapped between two value-systems - British and Indian. Her disillusionment arising out of her belief in English values is clearly reflected in her feelings when she says:

> Irreligious as I am I can't help being contemptuous of the laziness of western religions, and I can't help criticising myself for not being even a bad Hindu.[49]

At the root of her disregard for her anglicisation there lies the discriminatory treatment given to her by the British. For example, Lili's experience at the general hospital when she had been there to visit Miss Crane is illustrative of the fact that the Indians were not treated as their equals and, therefore, she says:

> .... but because I was an Indian I wasn't really allowed, anyway, not welcome.[50]

The same attitude is further pointed out by her when she says that 'the Europeans always looked on Indian titles as a bit of a joke.[51] It is not from the point of view of showing the love for nativism in Lili that Scott is presenting the disillusionment in this character, but by doing so he simply wants to show what may be called abnormal behaviour on her part.

Hari Kumar is presented as a victim of the evils of racial discrimination on the part of the British officials. Hari, a young Indian, who has been brought up in England and educated at one of its most prestigious public schools, develops a genuine love relationship with Daphne Manners transcending the racial barrier. After consummating their love, their sexual intercourse, in the Bibighar Gardens they are attacked by the gang of Indian hooligans who beat up Kumar and rape Daphne. Merrick, the police officer in charge of the case, tries to pin the crime on Kumar, but certain technical details and, most importantly, Daphne's refusal to give evidence that would implicate him, make it impossible to charge him with the offence. Nevertheless, he is detained in prison under Defence of the Realm ordinances, being 'suspected' by Merrick of subversive activities against the British during the disturbances. Thus, the character of Hari Kumar symbolises the atrocities of the Raj originating from the racial discriminations of the British officers in India. Caroline Moorehead points out that Scott has created the character of Hari Kumar out of his real experience. She believes that Scott's return visit to India in 1964, when he met the middle-class professional Indians he had never probably met before, 'jolted him back on course'.[52] However, the important thing to note is that Hari is a totally anglicised person who never knew the Indian way of life. His opinion regarding the All India Congress and its leaders is out and out anglicised. He doesn't believe in Congress claim that it represents the whole India.[53] His observation of various Indian national leaders reveals his anglicised position. In one of his letters to Colin Lindsey he points out the difference of opinion among the Indian leaders like Gandhi, Nehru and Subhas Bose. His appreciation of Churchill also reveals his anglicised position. In this respect he writes:

> The appearance of Churchill as head of the British war cabinet (greeted by the English here with such joy) has depressed the Indians. I expect they are being emotional about it. I'd no idea Churchill's name stank to this extent. They call him the arch-imperialist.[54]

Here we find that he does not appreciate the Indian leaders as he appreciates the British ones. As Hari goes on questioning Indian values and never challenging the British values Scott seems to sympathise with him. He is never critical of Kumar as he is that of Lili Chatterji. The point of anglicisation brings in the discussion of the character of Dulip Kumar, Hari's father. Like Lili, he is presented as an ambivalent character; his ambivalence emerging from his search for Indianness despite the fact that he was brought up in Western tradition. Dulip's experience of the British is that of a person of the subject race. Everything he does is treated as the conscious mimicry of the British for whom it was an object of ridicule. When he becomes conscious of this he says:

> It amused them mostly. Sometimes it irritated them. It still does. Never they could listen to us and forget that we were a subject, inferior people.[55]

When he returned from England he was treated as a 'halfman' -unclean by traditional Hindu standards and custom because he had crossed the black water. 'To purify himself he was persuaded to consume the five products of the cow which include the cow's dung and urine. Although, not, of course, the flesh' Scott criticises Dulip's character because, like Lili, he believes in the deeply rooted Indianness. Scott comments:

> The trouble was, Dulip thought, that India had made its mark on him and no subsequent experience would erase it. Beneath the thin layers of anglicisation was a thickness of Indianness that the arranged marriage had only confirmed and strengthened.[56]

At times, as rightly pointed out by Parry, Dulip Kumar, 'who acknowledges and resents his own deep-seated Indianness, is pathetically pro-English and his apostasy of all things Indian can be read as a statement of how the colonised can be deformed by the shame of their own culture induced by the rulers' disapprobation'.[57]

Mr Srinivasan, popularly known as Vassi, a Hindu lawyer from Mayapore, is depicted as a normal Indian character. The fact that he criticises the British attitude of equating Congress with Hinduism speaks of his belief in Indian secularism. In this context he says to the British visitors:

> Perhaps to you Congress is synonymous with Hindu. To us -originally - it was always the All India Congress - founded

incidentally by an Englishman. But since there have always been more Hindus than Muslims in India, it has also always gone without saying that its membership is and was predominantly Hindu.[58]

Srinivasan's Indianness is further illustrated when he points out the feeling of superiority among the British people not only during the Raj days but even after the Raj. He remarks about an Englishman:

And of course underneath all this there is this other thing, his natural distrust of us, his natural dislike of black people, the dislike he may think he hasn't got but soon finds he has when he's been out here a while, the distrust and dislike he shares with those old predecessors of his.[59]

Srinivasan, who has a deep respect for Indian culture, especially, the religious aspect of it, points out to the British visitors the reforms in the Indian temple. He states how the Indian government has implemented new policies that have cut down a lot the extortion that used to go on. Thus, his pride in the achievements of the Indian government is seen when he says:

This is one of the things we old Congressmen insisted on... that India should be a secular democratic state, not a priest-ridden autocracy.[60]

However, the Britishers do not show any interest in his views and go on pointing the ugly aspects of the Indian temple. Here also we notice Scott's condescending attitude towards India.

In the band of Indian characters Mr S.V. Vidyasagar, a journalist of the *Mayapore Gazette*, is, probably, a different character since he is shown as an active nationalist. In the course of his work as a journalist he becomes familiar with the British administration and the social life of the English people as well. Later on he resigns the *Mayapore Gazette* and takes up a new job with *Mayapore Hindu*. He describes how often they had to be alert and cautious as the activists. He writes:

In those days we had to be careful to avoid arrest unless of course one of us decided to seek arrest deliberately by open infringement of regulations. Also we had to be careful when choosing our friends or casual acquaintances. Many innocent-seeming fellows were police spies.[61]

This points out the difficulties the freedom fighters had to face during their struggle for Independence. Vidyasagar's strong belief in nationalist movement makes him prepared for any kind of sacrifice at the time of the rebellion in 1942. After he was arrested for printing seditious literature he was interrogated for hours to give information about "underground system", but he didn't, and consequently sentenced to two years rigorous imprisonment. The *Mayapore Hindu* was suppressed and offices closed down by order. Thus, the participation of Vidyasagar in freedom struggle throws light on the Indian nationalist movement and the harsh manner in which the British tried to suppress it. Though Scott is realistic in his delineation, he does it from the viewpoint of showing it as a main hurdle in the progress being made by the British in India. This shows Scott's strong belief in the values of the Raj which do not admit the feeling of nationalism among the colonized natives.

Scott's novelistic strategy involves the subtle portrayal of British characters. The most important British characters that appear in the novel are Miss Edwina Crane, Miss Daphne Manners, Lady Ethel Manners, Mr Ronald Merrick and Mr Robin White. The character of Miss Crane, the Supervisor of the Mayapore District's Protestant Mission Schools, is developed as a missionary teacher. Though the historical canon would not really be a criterion for the historical novelist, we cannot neglect Richard James' view which proves how Scott has made a good deal of research in case of the character. Mr James, who calls himself 'a child of the Raj', remembers meeting Miss Crane, a spinster missionary, though, of course, his Miss Crane, acted differently and said to him that Mr Gandhi was a good man. Here we can point out the British viewpoint of Scott in depicting this character. However, James' Miss Crane, like Scott's, also entertained young British soldiers.[62] Further he points out that the main intention of the novelist behind creating this character is to convey the Christian element of the Raj. Quite convincingly James states:

> She was a missionary. In India the Raj was meant to be Christian. Its underlying ethos was certainly Christian, and it worshipped at its garrison churches, manned by its ecclesiastical establishment. Paul Scott has marvellous vignettes of worship

at hill-station Pankot. But it was an essentially British affair;
and to try to spread your faith to the Indians.[63]

The missionary element forms the part of progressive ideas of Scott
regarding the Raj. Miss Crane's moral crisis, which reveals her character, can
be established from the change in her behaviour which is significant so far
as her role in British India is concerned. She removes Mr Gandhi's picture
from the walls of her study and no longer entertains Indian ladies to tea but
young English soldiers instead. Consequently the Indian ladies stop visiting
Edwina's bungalow, the act for which she takes Mr Gandhi a responsible
person. She dislikes Gandhi's policy of challenging the British rule in India
and hence distrusts him. In her mind regarding Gandhi's policy she finds the
British as better masters than anyone else. Before the Quit India Movement
(1942) she had great regard for Gandhi and had laughed at Europeans who
said that Gandhi was not to be trusted. But she changed her opinion when Mr
Gandhi had extended, she thought, 'what looked like an open invitation to
the Japanese to come and help him rid India of the British - and if he thought
that they would be the better masters then she could only assume he was out
of his senses, or which was worse, revealing that his philosophy of nonviolence
had a dark side that added upto total invalidation of its every aspect'.[64] Miss
Crane's critique of the Indian nationalist movement aims at pointing out
how it acted as 'spoiler' in the progress of the genuine relationship between
the British and the Indians. Her strong moral abilities are easily conveyed
when Scott presents her as a determined person. Even if it was a difficult job
to be in India she consciously accepts it and continues without bothering
the hardships in her way. In conversation as a nurse-companion to Mrs
Nesbitt-Smith on voyage to India, Mrs Smith says to her, "Good heavens.
Crane; what on earth has possessed you... you'd be with blacks and half-
castes, cut off from your own kind."[65] Here the derogatory language used
in case of the Indians shows that the Indians were treated as uncivilized by
the British. However, she remained firm on her determination. Operating in
this context, Scott provides Miss Crane with a considerable degree of moral
and physical courage. During the riots of 1942, in spite of the fact that she
knew the town was violent outside she along with Mr Chaudhuri went with
the school children to their houses. But on their way, unfortunately, she was
attacked by the rioters and her Indian colleague, Mr Chaudhuri was killed.

Scott has conveyed a full sense of the tragedy through her frustration. Crane's frustration is representative of the British who had wished that the day would come when their rule in India would end, not bloodily, but in peace. This violent act is symbolically presented. It symbolises the way in which the British rule was coming to an end. in the moments of her frustration she thinks:

> For years, for nearly a century, the books that Indians have read have been the books of our English radicals, our English liberals. There has been, you see, a seed. A seed planted in the Indian imagination and in the English imagination. Out of it was to come something sane and grave, full of dignity, full of thoughtfulness and kindness and peace and wisdom.[66]

These views are significant since they fully bring out Scott's point of view. The character of Miss Crane reveals his belief that it was only the progressive ideas of the British Raj that could have contributed a lot to the development of India, but, unfortunately, owing to the freedom struggle the task was left unfinished. In this respect Francine Weinbaum points out that 'though Edwina, embodying the values of the Raj, is attempting to achieve some form of union with or for India and Indians, tragically, the price of attempted union is some form of diminishment and she rarely doubts the rightness or value of the British goals'.[67] But it must be noted that it is only for the idealisation of the British values that Scott has created this character and, therefore, it probably lacks objective assessment.

Daphne Manners, who, after her parents' death, was brought up by Sir Henry and Lady Manners, was staying in Mayapore, at the house of Lili Chatterjee, plays a central role in the novel. To reveal the character of Miss Manners Scott makes an excellent use of the two letters she wrote to her aunt which Lady Manners afterwards gave to Lili Chatterjee and a 'journal' (April 1943) written by her addressed to Lady Manners. Through these objects it is made clear that Daphne is a liberal English, though, at times, critical of Indians. For example, in her first letter, dated 26th February 1942, she explicitly expresses her liberal views. They are evident when she expresses her resentment towards the policy of not allowing the Indians in the first class railway compartment. She refers to the incident when Nello Ghatterjee was turned out of a first class compartment by a couple of boxwallah Englishmen and says:

> It seems to me that if the railways allow an Indian to make a
> first class booking then no one should be able to stop them
> using what they're paid for.[68]

Her attitude is further illustrated in her feelings regarding Judge Menen, an old friend of Lili, whom she liked very much. Though he was much older than Robin White, the District Commissioner, it took a long time for him to rise to a position of authority only because he was an Indian. Her liberal attitude is also reflected when Lili's act of sponsoring her was not considered favourably by the British. When she was interviewed by Matron of the Civil Hospital she mentioned that Lili was her 'real' sponsor but Matron didn't like it since she believed that 'it was a 'British' general hospital where it was necessary to exclude all extraneous considerations'.[69] She didn't consider Lili as Daphne's sponsor and said that she had three sponsors - Mr Macintosh, herself (Matron) and her own surname, all the three being English. But Lili being an Indian was treated as extraneous. Thus, only because Daphne is liberal in her attitude she could expose the British idea of racial discrimination.

Daphne is quite consistent in her attitude towards the Indians which is seen when she protects Hari from Merrick's repeated attempts to charge Hari of rape. In her journal she clarifies that Hari was not guilty of the offence. On the contrary, it was Ranald Merrick, who, out of his racial hatred towards the Indians, took him as a convict. He never liked an English girl falling in love with an Indian. This discriminatory attitude in Merrick's character is very well discussed by Gomathi Narayanan in her archetypal study of the novel. In it she explains the rape of Daphne Manners in terms of the 'Prospero- Complex' which represents the psychological motif of colonization. The archetypal motif can be traced back in literature to Shakespeare's *The Tempest*, where, Prospero, the colonizer, accuses his native subject, Caliban, of having attempted to violate the honour of his daughter Miranda.[70] The theme of rape in this novel naturally makes us think of the same theme that appears in Forster's *A Passage to India*. There is a basic difference between Adela and Daphne as pointed out by Swinden. Adela's lie aims at accusing Dr. Aziz, on the contrary, in *The jewel in the Crown*, Daphne's is intended to defend Hari.[71] Thus, *A Passage to India* is altogether different from *The Jewel in the Crown*.

Daphne's liberal attitude is further noted when she says:

> I hate the impression we automatically get of things and places
> and people that make us say, for instance, "This is Indian.
> This is British."[72]

Again, it can be seen when she says to Merrick in connection with Hari:

> I said I'd be grateful if people would stop telling me who could
> be my friends and who not, and that I personally didn't care
> what colour people were, and it was obviously only Hari's
> colour, the fact that he was an Indian, that got people's goat.[73]

In spite of the fact that Daphne is a liberal English girl, her liberalism is not free from criticising the Indians which becomes clear in one of her letters, dated 7th July, 1942. She is critical of the middle class Indians who hoard foodstuffs in case of famine. About this and the corrupt nature of Indians she says:

> Jack Poulson says it's the curse of India, the way the middle-
> class and well-to-do Indians swoop into the stores the moment
> a crisis even threatens. But that's apparently nothing to the
> corruption that goes on in higher circles where bulk food-
> stuffs are handled.[74]

The point is further illustrated by Scott when he treats the entire Bibighar Gardens affair as symbolic of the British-Indian relationship, the symbol that represents India as a colonised country. Daphne remarks in this connection:

> Well, there has been more than one rape. I can't say, Auntie,
> that I lay back and enjoyed mine. But Lili was trying to lie back
> and enjoy what we've done to her country. I don't mean done in
> malice. Perhaps there was love. Oh, somewhere, in the past, and
> now, and in the future, love as there was between me and Hari.[75]

Thus, Daphne's symbolic remarks about the Indians who supported the British imperial power in India at the cost of their own identity, their own self-respect, express her criticism of the slavish mentality of the Indians.

The explanation of Merrick's role also becomes significant at this juncture because it is closely connected with the character of Daphne Manners. Basically Daphne believes in the British-Indian relationship as British having civilizing attitude towards Indians which can be useful only when there is a bond of love between the two. And hence she attacks the Merricks who, with their insular attitude, spoilt this relationship. She, therefore, says:

> But the spoilers are always there, aren't they? The Swinsons. The bitches who travelled as far as Lahore. The Ronald Merricks.[76]

Max Beloff's analysis of the character of Merrick is in keeping with that of Daphne Manners. Beloff holds that 'it is true that the central incident in the story is its crystallising factor. *Foe,* in his prosecution of Kumar, the policeman Merrick-reveals how personal feelings of class as well as of race - unlike Kumar Merrick is not "a gentleman" - can distort and envenom what should be the process of imperial justice'.[77] John Mellors' description of Merrick as 'a crazy-mixed-up villain with sexual, racial and political obsessions'[78] seems to be a generalised one since as pointed out by Weinbaum, the "Villain" is not the British policeman Ronald Merrick so much as the force of insularity which victimizes protagonists and antagonists alike. Whether in politics or human relations, the enemies of love are self-interest and barriers to communication, insular forces apparent in "the white robot", the system of the British Raj that destroyed the union of Hari Kumar and Daphne Manners'.[79] Thus the character of Merrick is important individually, but more important of the system of which he is the product. The character of Ronald Merrick, as presented in this volume, appears to be a negative one against the backdrop of liberal values adopted by the British. His character is further developed in the second volume, *The Day of the Scorpion*, which we will analyse in our discussion later.

Ethel Manners, Daphne's aunt, who, like Daphne and Miss Crane, appears to be justifying Scott's viewpoint, is revealed through the letters written by her to Lili Chatterjee in which she tells about Parvati, Daphne's daughter. The letters also tell us that after the rape Daphne went to Kashmir to stay with her aunt, but, unfortunately, died intestate. In one of her letters to Lili, dated August 5, 1947, she regrets the partition of India since it was not the aim of British imperial power - the thought that represents Scott's point of view towards the partition of India. Her belief that 'their only justification for two hundred years of power was unification shows, according to Scott, the progressive nature of the British Raj.[80] She expresses her views regarding the constitution of free India in the following words:

> Won't that constitution be a sort of love letter to the English -
> the kind an abandoned lover writes when the affair has ended
> in what passes at the time as civilized and dignified mutual
> recognition of incompatibility.[81]

As compared to the male characters Scott's female characters are more fascinating. Benita Parry rightly points out:

> It is Scott's sibylline old white women who, in so acting out
> their personal disillusion, signal a larger social failure which
> for Scott is the ending of an era in which the British role in
> India had been viable and valuable.[82]

The minor characters of Robin White and Brigadier Reid, both of them being in the administrative services of the Raj, are developed against the background of Indian political situation. The character of Brigadier Reid, DSO, MC, is revealed through the Edited Extracts from the unpublished memoirs of him. Reid's memoirs bring to our mind the increasing unrest in India when he arrived in Mayapore in 1942. This period is the most crucial period in the history of modern India and Scott, by describing a vital aspect of that period, exemplifies Bruce Lancaster's observation about one of the characteristics of the historical novel. He says:

> The historical novel must be laid at some crucial time in a
> nation's history. It will probably embrace some form of strife,
> for crises usually engender violence. And the crises must be
> removed in time from the experience of the bulk of living
> readers, else it falls into mere reporting.[83]

In the period of turbulance Reid was much worried about the safety of the British people in India and that is why he decides to bring the Brigade's British battalion - the Berkshires -into Mayapore. His intention is clearly revealed in the following words:

In bringing the Berkshires into Mayapore I was also not unaware of the good effect this world would have on our own people there - men and women doing difficult jobs at a time of special crisis.[84]

As Reid holds Gandhi responsible for the crisis, it helps in understanding his point of view towards the Indian national movement for independence. He believes that after the failure of the Cripps Mission in April 1942 Gandhi launched his famous Quit India campaign which looked to the British like an invitation to the Emperor of Japan to walk in and take over the reins of government. Upon this he thinks that 'Mr Gandhi's policy of non-violent non-co-operation was a policy that could bring the country to a standstill'.[85] This brings out Scott's view that Gandhi was the person who obstructed the progress of India. This brings out Scott's viewpoint as colonizer.

Reid's views regarding the British concept of federal government also represent Scott's point of view:

The act of 1935 which envisaged a federal government at the centre, representative of all walks of Indian life, and elected states governments in the provinces, seemed to a man like myself (who had everything to lose and nothing to gain by Indian Independence) a statesmanlike, indeed noble concept, on that Britain could have been proud of us as a fitting end to a glorious chapter in her imperial history.[86]

Reid believes that initially it was a part of progressive nature of the British imperial policy; but the plan was frustrated by the All India Congress and hence he criticises it. At the time of the War Congress members of central assembly had walked out to protest against the sending of Indian Troops to the Middle East and Singapore. Similarly, the Congress Ministers in the provinces had resigned because the Viceroy had declared war without consulting them. He calls this action as a sign of the political immaturity. His frustration is highlighted when he believes that, unfortunately, 'this scheme led only to a scramble for power and it failed and the heartrending cries for freedom sounded hollow in retrospect as one watched the scramble and listened to the squabbles that broke out between Hindus, Muslims, Sikhs, Princes and others'.

It reflects Scott's views that Indians were not fit to run their own government and therefore, all the chaos was found after achieving the freedom.

Mr Reid correlates the two dastardly attacks on English women, the first upon Miss Crane and the second on Miss Manners, to the effect of the activities of the Congress. It brings out the historical significance of the novel. In his account, Reid's mention of Merrick's views regarding Gandhi represents his views. He records:

> Merrick described Gandhi on this occasion (when we drank a hasty cup of tea together) as a "crazy old man" who had completely lost touch with the people he thought he still led, and so was the dupe of his own "dreams and crazy illusions," and had no idea how much he was laughed at by the kind of young men, he, Merrick, had to keep in order.[87]

Thus by negating the great Indian nationalist leaders like Gandhi he aims at saying how good was the presence of British in India.

The character of Robin White is revealed through an edited transcript of written and spoken comments by Robin White himself. In this respect Parry's analysis of White is worth taking into account since she has pointed out that though he was a liberal British officer basically he believed in the progressive values of the Raj. How White enjoyed the privileged position is pointed out by Parry as follows:

> In his recollections Robin White, CIS, ICS, Retired, a serious and humane man, not given to bombast about morality, looks back on the raj as exploitation tempered by "the onus of moral leadership" (Vol. 1: p. 317). [88]

Thus, through his character Scott has illustrated the Raj values of responsibility and privilege. His belief in the Raj is further illustrated in his distrust in Gandhi whom he describes as follows:

> I certainly distrusted Gandhi - but not in the way Reid, for instance, distrusted him. I distrusted Gandhi because I couldn't see how a man who wielded such power and influence

could remain uninhibited by it, and always make the right decisions for the right reasons.[89]

According to him, it was not from social awareness that Gandhi identified himself with the outcastes of the Hindu religion but he believes that the caste system probably had a truly religious significance for him in those days. Gandhi's going to England was significant only in terms of his worldly ambition. No man is without ambition, but perhaps few men, have been forced to doubt the power for good that ambition represents as much as Gandhi was forced to do. He felt in the end that he was working out a personal salvation in public all the time.[90] Scott's point of view as revealed in depicting Gandhi's character can very well be apprehended by comparing him with Indo-Anglian writers who looked at Gandhi as a great national leader. In *The Sword and the Sickle* (1942), M. Anand has portrayed Lalu Singh as a propagator of Mahatma Gandhi or in K.S. Venkatramani' s *Kandan, the Patriot* (1932), Kandan is shown as an exponent of Gandhian politics. It reflects the national movement for political freedom under the leadership of Gandhi, though Gandhi himself is not introduced in the novel. Again in *Kanthapura* (1938), the image of Gandhi as depicted by Raja Rao is totally different from that of Scott. For instance, the narrator of *Kanthapura* refers to Gandhi as Rama and says:

> They say the Mahatma will go to the redmen's country and will get us swaraj. He will bring us swaraj, the Mahatma. And we shall all be happy. And Rama will come back from exile, and Seeta will be with him, for Ravana will be slain and Seeta freed.[91]

Thus, the image of Gandhi as a saviour as depicted by the Indo-Anglian writers is opposite to that of Scott's.

Scott has made a marvellous use of the technique of comparison between the pre- and post-Independence India, so as to justify the moral aspect of the British Raj. In their visit to an Indian temple after almost twenty five years, the British tourists note the poverty-stricken surroundings of the temple in the following manner: 'there are a cow or two, parked cycle-rickshaws, many people and several beggar women who converge upon the studebaker, carrying sleeping children aslant their bangled arms. The tourist says that to look straight in the eyes of a beggar woman would be fatal. "In India the head too often has to be turned away."[92] Scott means to say that after almost twentyfive years of self -rule Indians have not been able to make progress. It is also seen when Scott points out Lili's discontent of the present Indian situation. Scott's intention is to show that it is not this India that the British expected. Hence Lili says:

> I suppose we are still waiting for the Mahatma because the previous one disappointed and surprised us by becoming a saint and martyr in the Western sense when that silly boy shot him. I'm sure there's a lesson in that for us. If the old man were alive today I believe he'd dot us all one on the head with his spinning-wheel and point out that if we go as we are we shall end up believing in saints.[93]

In this way, the use of past-present relationship becomes a significant aspect of Scott's novel which exemplifies Fleishman's view:

> The men of the present look back to the men of the past not merely to understand them but to understand themselves; historical thought is seen here as moving from the present to the past in order to be reflected back to the present with enhanced power of meeting the problems of life.[94]

This technique is further used when Scott makes use of a room in the MacGregor House where the tourist finds 'pouffes and purses scattered round the room, curiously dry and lifeless, like sea-weed taken from its element'. The room is also capable of bringing to the nose of a knowledgeable traveller the recollected smell of oil and water'. At this stage he points out the faint stagnation that seems to surround a big ship directly it stops moving. The writer compares this situation of stagnation with that of India and says that India also seems to be at anchor.[95] Or this can be seen in the observations of Mr Laxminarayan who is now writing a history of the origins of Indian nationalism. When the British tourist visits him he says:

> They are not interested in the past and neither are we except to the extent that we wonder what the fuss was about and aren't sure that our own government is doing any better, or

even that it is a government that represents us. It seems to be the government of an uneasy marriage between old orthodoxy and old revolutionaries, and such people have nothing to say to us that we want to hear.[96]

It all consolidates Scott's view that even after a considerable period of almost twentyfive years of self-rule Indians have not been able to achieve anything dignified and implicitly means that it would have been a different picture had the British continued in India; but the Indian's aspirations for the self-rule kept them away from the progress which was the department of the British Raj only. In this way, "Scott's progressive outlook towards the Raj makes him believe that the world for which the Raj prepared India is not the one in which she struggles to survive. This again represents the views of Scott as colonizer.

NOTES AND REFERENCES

1   The simplistic comparative view can be found in quite a few articles; to quote but two of them: (i) Nancy W. Ross, "Paul Scott; Unsung Singer of Hindustan", *Saturday Review*, June 24, 1974, p. 58, and (ii) C.W. Mann, review of *The Jewel in the Crown,* by Paul Scott, *Library Journal*, July 17, 1966, p. 4703. Writing about this comparative tendency of the critics Manohar Malgonkar, a close friend of Scott, mentions how Scott protested against this tendency in his obitury on Scott, "Salute to Paul Scott," <u>Debonair</u>, May 5, 1978, that one thing Paul Scott always protested against was the tendency of the critics to compare him to E.M. Forster. The seriousness in this can be understood when Malgonkar politely admits that Paul would have forgiven him for linking his name with that of Forster, though, of course, he shows this link only to point out that both of them shared, besides their love for India, that rarest of attributes, of being truly civilized persons.

2   Paul Scott, "India: A Post-Forsterian View" Mary Stocks (Ed.) *Essays by Divers Hands*, Vol. XXXVI (London: OUP, 1970), p. 117.

3   *Ibid.*

4   Paul Gray, "Comic Coda to a Song of India," Review of Staying On by Paul Scott, *Time,* 110:89, July 18, 1977, p. 46.

5   Paul Scott, *The Jewel in the Crown* (Frogmore: Panther Books, Ltd., 1966), p. 10.

6   Herbert Butterfield, *The Historical Novel* (Cambridge: OUP, 1924), p. 21.

7   Paul Scott, *The Jewel in the Crown* (Frogmore: Panther Books Ltd., 1966), p. 9.

8   *Ibid.*

9   Martin Levin, Review of *The Jewel in the Crown*, by P. Scott, *New York Times Book Review,* July 17, 1966, p. 28.

10 Paul Scott, *The Jewel in the Crown* (Frogmore: Panther Books Ltd., 1966), p. 136.

11 *Ibid.,* p. 242.

12 *Ibid.,* p. 243.

13 *Ibid.,* p. 346.

14 E.M. Forster, *The Hill of Devi* (London, 1953), p. 39.

15 E.M. Forster, *A Passage to India* (London: Penguin, 1924), p. 68.

16   Paul Scott, *The jewel in the Crown* (Frogrnore: Panther Books Ltd., 1966), pp. 17-18.

17   *Ibid.,-*pp. 34-35.

18   E.M.. Forster, *A Passage to India* (London: Penguin, 1924), p. 10.

19   *Ibid.*, p. 18.

20   John Mellors, "Raj Mahal: Paul Scott's India Quartet," *London Magazine*, Vol. 15, No. 2, June, July, 1975, p. 63.

21   Paul Scott, *The Jewel in the Crown* (Frogmore: Panther Books Ltd., 1966), p. 18.

22   *Ibid.*, p. 20.

23   *Ibid.*, p. 21.

24   *Ibid.*, p. 37.

25   *Ibid.*, p. 54.

26   *Ibid.*, p. 213.

27   *Ibid.*, p. 217.

28   *Ibid.*, p. 52.

29   *Ibid.*, p. 189.

30   *Ibid.*, p. 228.

31   Meena Shirwadkar, *Image of Woman in Indo-Anglian Novel*, (New Delhi: Sterling Publishing House Pvt. Ltd., 1979), pp. 6-7.

32   Paul Scott, *The Jewel in the Crown* (Frogmore: Panther Books Ltd., 1966), p. 75.

33   Benita Parry, "Paul Scott's Raj," *South Asian Review*, Vol. 8, No. 4, July, October, 1975, p. 364.

34   Patrick Swinden, *Paul Scott: Images of India* (London: Macmillan Press Ltd., 1980), pp. 79-80.

35   Paul Scott, *The Jewel in the Crown* (Frogmore: Fanther Books Pvt. Ltd., 1966), pp. 26-27.

36   *Ibid.*, p. 27.

37   *Ibid.*, p. 28.

38   Benita Parry, "Paul Scott's Raj," *South Asian Review'*, Vol. 8, No.4 July-October, 1975, p. 36 2.

39   George Orwell, *Burmese Days* (London: Penguin, 1975), p.17

40   Paul Scott, *The Jewel in the Crown* (Frogmore: Panther Books Ltd., 1966), p. 115,

41   *Ibid.*, p. 181.

42   *Ibid.*, pp. 180-181.

43   *Ibid.*, p. 174.

44   *Ibid.*, p. 172.

45   *Ibid.*, p. 173.

46   Avrom Fleishman, *The English Historical Novel: Walter Scott to Virginia Woolf* (Baltimore and London: Johns Hopkins Press, 1977), p. 10.

47   Paul Scott, *The Jewel in the Crown* (Frogmore: Panther Books, 1966), p. 139.

48   *Ibid.*, p. 146.

49   *Ibid.*, p. 78,

50   Ibid., p. 88.

51   *Ibid.*, p. 91.

52   Caroline Moorehead, "Novelist Paul Scott: Getting Engrossed in the Death-Throes of the Raj," *Times*, 20 October, 1975, a Times Profile.

53   Paul Scott, *The Jewel in the Crown* (Frogmore: Panther Books, 1966), p. 270.

54   *Ibid.*, p. 275.

55   *Ibid.*, p. 215.

56   *Ibid.*, p. 225.

57   Benita Parry, "Paul Scott's Raj," *South Asian Review*, Vol. 8, No. 4, July-Oct. 1975, p. 367.

58   Paul Scott, *The Jewel in the Crown* (Frogmore: Panther Books, 1966), p. 199.

59   *Ibid.*, p. 203.

60   *Ibid.*, p. 207.

61   *Ibid.*, pp. 362-63.

62   Richard James, "In the Steps of Paul Scott," *The Listner,*8 March 1979, pp. 359-60.

63   *Ibid.*

64   Paul Scott, *The Jewel in the Crown* (Frogmore: Panther Books, 1966), p. lo.

65   *Ibid.*, p. 21.

66   *Ibid.*, p. 72.

67   Francine Weinbaum, "Paul Scott's India: *The Raj Quartet,*" *Critique*, 20:1 (1979), p. 103.

68 Paul Scott, *The Jewel in the Crown* (Frogmore: Panther Books, 1966), p. 104.

69 *Ibid.*, p. 106.

70 Gomathi Narayanan, "Paul Scott's Indian Quartet: The Story of a Rape," *The Literary Criterion*, Vol. XII, No. 4, 1978, p. 47.

71 Patrick Swinden, *Paul Scott, Images of India* (London: Macmillan, 1980), p. 82.

72 Paul Scott, *The Jewel in the Crown* (Frogmore: Panther Books, 1966), p. 413.

73 *Ibid.*, p. 417.

74 *Ibid.*, p. 109.

75 *Ibid.*, p. 462.

76 *Ibid.*

77 Max Beloff, "The End of the Raj: Paul Scott's Novels as History," *Encounter*, Vol. XLVI, No. 5, May 1976, p. 67.

78 John Mellors, "Raj Mahal: Paul Scott's India Quartet," *London Magazine*, Vol. 15, No. 2, June, July 197 5, p.63.

79 Francine Weinbaum, "Paul Scott's India: *The Raj Quartet*," *Critique*, 20:1 (1979), p. 104.

80 Paul Scott, *The Jewel in the Crown* (Frogmore: Panther Books, 1966), p. 473.

81 *Ibid.*, p. 476.

82 Benita Parry, "Paul Scott's Raj, *South Asian Review*, Vol. 8, No. 4, July, October, 1975, pp. 360-61.

83 Bruce Lancaster, "The Insides of a Novel," *The Atlantic Monthly,* February 1946, p. 75.

84 Paul Scott, *The Jewel in the Crown* (Frogmore: Panther Books, 1966), p. 287.

85 *Ibid.*

86 *Ibid.*, p. 288.

87 *Ibid.*, p. 318.

88 Benita Parry, "Paul Scott's Raj," *South Asia- Review,* Vol. 8, No. 4, July, October 1975, p. 362.

89 Paul Scott, *The Jewel in the Crown* (Frogmore: Panther Books, 1966), p. 341.

90 *Ibid.*, p. 344.

91 Raja Rao, *Kanthapura* (London: Allen and Unwin, 1933), (Delhi: Hind Pocket Books, n.d.), p. 257.

92 Paul Scott, *The Jewel in the Crown* (Frogmore: Panther Books, 1966), p. 205.

93 *Ibid.,* p. 79.

94 Avrom Fleishman, *The English Historical Novel* (Baltimore The Johns Hopkins Press, 2nd ed.-, 1972), pp. 13-14.

95 Paul Scott, *The Jewel in the Crown* (Frogmore: Panther Books, 1966), p. 81.

96 *Ibid.,* p. 265.

2. *The Day of the Scorpion*

The Day of the Scorpion (1968)

The Day of the Scorpion (1968), the second novel in *The Raj Quartet*, is, as pointed out by Mr S.L. Hopkinson, really the story of the twilight of the British rule in India shown mainly from the British point in which the real heroine is, of course. India as she passes from one epoch to another'.[1] More specifically, in the words of Keith Walker, 'it shows through an established Anglo-Indian family how the old balance between ruler and ruled is disrupted by the war and the appearance on the scene of a new type of Englishman'.[2] Within this point of reference, it is my attempt to study Scott's statement on the twilight days of the British Raj. At the outset it is to be noted that Scott's vision constitutes the actual historical happenings which cannot be separated from the social reality of the times. It implies the belief that since Indians need a good deals of progress on the social scale they should not be granted self-rule until they are fit for that. According to Scott, the British task remained unfinished due to the untimely freedom granted to India. And hence he takes the stance of justifying the moral side of the British. Further, it is to be noted that the same pattern as in *The Jewel* is followed in the second volume as well: the recreation of the past with the help of effective symbols consisting of objects and places and tragic situations that reveal Scott's point of view.

As has been already observed, the technique of past-present relationship is one of the important features of the historical novel. To put it in the words of Mr Pearce:

> ...historicism assumes that the past, by virtue of its very pastness, becomes an aspect of the present. In effect, a literary work carries the past into the present.[3]

However, the use of this technique is found only in the Prologue of this novel whereas in the case of *The Jewel* he uses it throughout the novel. In the Prologue the past is recreated mainly by focusing on a place called Ranpur. After twenty five years of the British exodus from India an Englishman, in his return visit to India, is searching for points of present contact with the reality of twenty five years ago. His impression of the town of Ranpur certainly has the undertone of the pride of the English. His visit to the town makes him feel that the people from the small and distant island of Britain, who built and settled there were attempting to express in the architectural terms their extraordinary talent for running things and making them work. Here his observation is significant to note. He says:

> If you look in places like Ranpur for evidence of things the British left behind which were of value, you might choose any one or several of the public works and installations as visible proof of them: the roads and railways and telegraph for a modern system of communication, the High Court for a sophisticated code of civil and criminal law, the college for education to university standard, the state Legislature for democratic government, the Secretariat for a civil service made in the complex image of that in Whitehall, the clubs for a pattern of urbane and civilized behaviour, the messes and barracks for an ideal of military service to the mother country.[4]

What impresses him in this respect is something for which there is no memorial but to which all these things collectively bear witness. Thus, whatever good things in India we see today they are attributed to the British Raj and in this manner it is shown that the past is inseparable from the present. This again reflects Scott's pride in English superiority.

The point is further illustrated through Scott's views regarding the decadence of Mohammedanism in India. At the beginning of the novel, we find the description of a Muslim woman whom the writer encounters in his return visit. Scott is critical of the woman because she wears the burkha, 'that unhygienic head-to-toe covering that turns a woman into a walking symbol of inefficient civic refuse collection and leaves you without even an impression of her eyes behind the slits she watches the gay world through, tempted but not tempting; a garment in all probability inflaming to her passions but chilling to her expectations of having them satisfied.[5] Similarly, Scott is critical of the woman for her habit, in spite of her poverty, of buying expensive things like scents, doesn't matter whether they are bought on loan. His criticism of the decadent Muslim religious values can be seen in the following words:

> ... the other mosques of Ranpur are no longer in use as houses of worship. Some of them have decayed, others less ruinous are used as store rooms by the Municipality. There are still Muslims in Ranpur but the days are gone when the

great festivals of the Id-al-fitr and id-al-Adza could fill the mosques with thousands of the faithful from the city and the surrounding villages of the plain.[6]

This comparison of present with the past aims at pointing out the bygone glory of the British Raj. Thus, Scott's idea of progress in history involves the presentation of historical changes in a linear way. In continuation with the Muslims in the Raj here he presents the Muslims in free India and points out their decadence. One thing is strikingly noticeable here that Scott, unlike most of the British, does not favour the Muslims. For example, how the British were in favour of Muslims is stated by Viscount Morley:

> I am an Occidental, not an Oriental... I think I like Indian Mohammedans, but I cannot go much further in an easterly direction.[7]

The explanation of this favouritism can be found probably in the similarities between the ways of living of the Muslims and Christians which went some way in making the British feel more at home with the Muslims than with the Hindus. However, Scott doesn't make any distinction between Hindus and Muslims in his attitude towards them.

The image of India and the Indians as presented in this novel is not much different from that in *The Jewel*, which means, it has all the bearing of Kiplingesque manner. For example, when he describes the city of Mirat of 1943 he points out how the structure of the city maintained the Hindu-Muslim distinction. In the city there was the Hindu Boys' College, an institution which owed its existence to Count Bronowsky, a Russian emigre, the Wazir of the Nawab of Mirat. Though in minority, a mere twenty per cent of the population, the Muslims of Mirat had a firm grip on the administration since the days of the Moghuls. Until Bronowsky's day few Hindus had held any public post of any importance. There were more mosques than temples, not because the rich Hindus of Mirat were unready to build temples but because permission to build was more often refused than granted.[8] Thus, the description of the city of Mirat vividly points out the rift between Hindus and Muslims. In this connection Scott is further trying to bring out how Muslims regarded religion more important than the formal education. He writes:

For the Muslim children an Academy of Higher Education had been established in the late nineteenth century, but its record was poor; there was a saying that a boy left there with no qualifications except for reciting passages from the Koran.[9]

Scott's consideration of Indian culture as outlandish makes him critical of it. In Lady Manners' attitude towards her servant Suleiman, for instance, it is seen how the British looked towards Indians as backward people. She says to Suleiman:

You had one wife we knew about and two concubines you pretended were your wife's sisters. And were a rogue and rake, and had children. God knows how many, by whom, nor where scattered.[10]

The Indians are also attacked in a distressing scene on the station platform where Merrick was solicited by an Indian woman in a white saree, probably Hari's aunt. She pleaded with him, fell on her knees and placed her forehead on the ground before his feet - the scene recalling Merrick's treatment of Hari Kumar. However, she was neglected by Merrick and was taken away by a certain man. Merrick believed that the man who attended her was only pretending and didn't care a fig for her. Merrick believes that his selfish motive only guided him to act like that. Therefore, he says:

It's sheer pretence. The case is useful to him, that's all. It serves his purpose. But that's India for you. They're quite indifferent to one another's sufferings when it comes down to it.[11]

Here we find Scott's attitude as a colonizer towards India. The references to Indian poverty are also to be noted. For instance, on their way to the Kandipat jail where Hari was kept Captain Rowan and Lady Manners notice the dirt and poverty in India which is described as follows:

They had entered a semi-rural area of hovels. There was a smell of human and animal excrement. A naked ash-smeared Sadhu leaned against a parapet and watched them go past, his arms folded, his head tilted. She saw his mouth open and his neck muscles swell, but could not distinguish his shout above the shouting of little boys who ran alongside the car calling for baksheesh.[12]

During the course of Hari's investigation by Rowan the anti-British Indians like Vidyasagar are ridiculed. They are ludicrous in the eyes of the British because:

> They were always laughing at the English. They pretended to hate them. But everything about their way of life was an aping of the English manner. The way they dressed, the style of slang, the things they'd learned.[13]

The slavish mentality of the Indians, as pointed out by Clark, speaks of the colonial attitude of an Englishman towards India. Clark's belief that the Indians have no history of their own is no more than the attitude of a colonial ruler. He says:

> Out here you've always had the negative side,' the reactionaries and the counter revolutionaries, but you've never had the bloody revolution. That's why an Indian urban dweller's life expectation is still thirty five and why people die of starvation while the band plays at Government House, and Pyari plays the Sitar at Mira's.[14]

The depiction of the Princedom of Mirat also throws light on the British Indian history. The relationship between the native princes and the British is illustrated through their treatment of the Nawab of Mirat. How the state was dominated by the Muslims and the British is quite evident in the description of the city of Mirat:

> There were two Mirats: the Mirat of palaces, mosques, minarets, and crowded bazaars, and the Mirat of open spaces, barracks, trees, and geometrically laid out roads with names like Wellesley, Gunnery and Mess.[15]

The Muslim domination is pointed out by referring to a lake to the south of Mirat which was adopted as a symbol of Nawab's power, of his fertility, of an assured succession reaching into the far distant future. The Muslim domination is seen when he says that in spite of the Hindu majority in the city they were not given much importance by the Muslims. It went to the extent that the mullahs declared the lake blessed by Allah, and the Hindus - eighty per cent of the population - were prohibited from using it even during the festival of Divali.[16] A few things throw light on the British-Indian princes relationship. The fact that a guest house in the European Palladian style was built in the late nineteenth century, round about the time that a British military cantonment was established with the Nawab's approval in the area north of the lake proves that the Nawab had healthy relations with the British. This becomes clear when he offers his guest house to the Laytons at the time of the wedding of Susan and Captain Teddie Bingham. Scott is quite authentic in depicting this type of relationship because of the fact that the princes were loyal to the crown as the crown protected their rights and privileges.[17] It follows that due to the ruled-ruler relationship the British did not treat Nawabs as their equals, the fact that is noticed when the Nawab visited the Laytons on the occasion of the wedding reception. When he reached there, he, not being an English, was prohibited from entering the reception room. And though it was an insulting treatment to the Nawab he didn't go away from the place but waited at the gate and later when taken in attended the function. Thus, in one of the talks between Merrick and Bronowsky there is a comment on the Indian princes' insignificant role in India:

> The Indian states are an anachronism too. The rubber-stamp
> administrator or executive is too advanced an animal for
> us, although ideally that is the likeness one looks for in the
> outward appearance.[18]

It indicates the decadence of the Indian princes which is, historically, quite an authentic phenomenon. However, the attitude of the British towards the princes reveals their belief in British superiority.

Most of the recreation of Anglo-India is done by using the places like Ranpur and Pankot. The history of these places brings to our mind the British style of life in India. In India the English people had two different places to live in for the summer and winter seasons. Ranpur was the permanent cool weather station of Colonel Layton's regiment, the 1st Pankot Rifles. Their hot weather station was in the hills of Pankot itself, a place to which the provincial government also moved during the summer. From April to September Pankot lived a full social life. The fact that the British had little knowledge of the area where Indians lived indicates that they did maintain a certain distance between the rulers and the ruled. To British, Pankot was the area where there were the clubs, the administrative quarters, the golf course, etc.

The Anglo-Indian past is also revived through the description of the Rose Cottage, the place where Mabel Layton, Sarah's grandmother, stayed with Barbara Batchelor, a retired mission school teacher. 'The cottage was one of the oldest in Pankot, built before the fashion came for building in a style more reminiscent of home. Stuccoed, whitewashed, with square columns on the verandahs and high ceilinged rooms inside, it was a piece of old Anglo-India, a bungalow with a large square entrance hall. The hall was panelled. Upon the polished wood Mabel's brass and copper shone. The bowls of flowers gave off a deep and dusty scent, and Sarah, standing in the doorway, half-closed her eyes and imagined the drone of bees on a summer's day at home in England, which she had thought of a Pankot in miniature. But England was far away and Pankot was miniature itself'.[19] The description is important because it shows their affluent style of living and the alienation from the English as well as the Indians.

As far as Indian characters are concerned one notices that fundamentally the British looked towards the Indians from the point of view of the rulers which becomes quite clear when Hari says, in respect of Merrick, that 'it wasn't enough to say Merrick was English and he was Indian but that Merrick was a ruler and he was one of the ruled'.[20] One of the most important characters that emerges in the novel is Mohammed Ali Kasim, popularly known as MAK. MAK represents the aspirations of the Indians for self rule and is, as pointed out by the *Times Literary Supplement* reviewer, 'a serious, strong, idealistic, humane, not at all unmindful of the benefits conferred by the British on India during the long hegemony'.[21] The story of MAK revives the turbulent period of 1942 which becomes an important aspect of Scott's historical imagination. After MAK, the Ex-Chief Minister, was arrested at his home in Ranpur at 5 a.m. on August 9th, 1942, under the Defence of India Rules there followed a meeting between him and the Governor of the province, Sir George Malcolm. The meeting throws light on the aspirations of the Indian nationalists represented by MAK. Kasim's staunch belief in nationalism is proved when he denies Malcolm's plea to resign the All India

Congress Committee and accept his offer to be the member of his executive council. He is shown such a resolute nationalist who believed in the unity of India that he had incurred the displeasure of Mr Jinnah who then had vision of a separate Muslim state.

Though Mr Kasim is shown as a staunch nationalist he is also shown as a person who has faith in British values and sincerity which throws light on Scott's belief in British superiority. It can be judged from the fact that he doesn't oppose Syed, his elder son, having taken King's Commission, Moreover, he feels it necessary for the future benefit of India which is clearly stated in these lines:

> The world is full of fools who don't see an inch in front of their noses. What kind of independence will it be when we get it if can't defend it? And how shall we be able to defend it if there aren't boys like Syed. willing to train and discipline themselves faithfully and steadfastly to inherit that side of our national responsibility?[22]

Thus Mr Kasim's belief in British values proves the superiority of the British as rulers who had something valuable to pass on to the Indians without which it was difficult for the Indians to have a self rule. In this manner, the character of MAK is developed to suit the author's point of view. Here we must note that the nationalist characters as depicted by Indian authors take the stance of rejecting the British values. For example, in K.S. Venkatramani's *Kandan, the Patriot,* Kandan, the leader of the freedom struggle in a village called Akkur, gives up his ICS in the probation period and joins the Indian national movement. Or in *Tomorrow is Ours* K.A. Abbas depicts a lawyer of Allahabad who joins the Non-co-operation Movement launched in 1920, giving up his lucrative practice, and suffers imprisonment and ultimately dies when jail diet tells upon his health. Unlike Scott, the nationalist characters as depicted by Indian authors take the stance of complete rejection of the British rule and strong belief in native values.

This point can further be seen in the ludicrous treatment given to Pandit Baba who first appeared in *The Jewel.* The meeting between Ahmed, Kasim's younger son, Social Secretary to the Nawab of Mirat and Pandit Baba, who is slippery, unscrupulous and bland,[23] points out the Indians' strong belief in their native traditions, similar to feeling of patriotism. When Ahmed started talking to him in English Pandit Baba didn't like it and retorted whether he did not feel shame to speak in the language of a foreign power, the language of his father's jailers.[24] The author's point that there was not any other language that can substitute English contributes to the fact that he is thinking from the British point of view. By sarcastically commenting on Pandit Baba he is narrating the importance of the English language in the following words:

> The Pandit was obviously proud of his facility. His refusal so far to speak in English did not mean he spoke it badly or was not proud of understanding and being able to speak it, but it was fashionable among Hindus of Baba's kind to decry it, to declare that once the British had been got rid of their language must go with them; although what would be placed in its place was difficult to tell. Even Pandit Baba Sahib would fare badly if he went out into some of the villages around Mirat and tried to understand what was said to him. He would need an interpreter, as most officials did. And the odds were the interpreter would interpret the local dialect in the language and the idiom of the British.[25]

Once Pandit Baba is ridiculed his views regarding patriotism are also rendered meaningless.

Scott ridicules Pandit Baba because, according to him, it is the nationalistic attitude of the Indians which is responsible for their backwardness. The characters of Pandit Baba and MAK are the only Indian characters that are developed to some extent in the novel.

However, the novel is extensively depicts the British characters. Most of the British characters are closely associated with the Layton family in India. The history of the Layton family is of immense importance since, as pointed out by Patrick Swinden, in this novel 'what Scott is preoccupied with is the effect the loss of India had on the Anglo-Indian community, on people like the Laytons and the families in whose circles they move in Mayapore, Ranpur and Pankot.'[26] The entire history of the Laytons narrated by Scott gives a historical dimension to the novel as it illustrates the tragedy the British in India had to face due to the historical force of World War II. It clearly points out that Scott's preoccupation is mainly with the sufferings of the British.

The tragedy begins with Mabel Layton, John's step mother, whose both husbands, one after another, were killed while in Indian service. Scott's main purpose behind the creation of this character is to point out the paternal attitude of the British which according to Scott, forms one of the important characteristics of the progressive nature of the British Raj. Her paternalism is revealed at the time of the collection of the General Dyer Fund. When the total sum collected for General Dyer was heard to have reached the substantial figure of £ 26,000 the ladies of Pankot and Ranpur felt justified. However, Mabel sent a cheque of £ 100 to the fund the Indians were raising for the families of Jallianwallah victims. Though her explanation for this act reveals her viewpoint of paternalism, it clearly brings out the idea of racial discrimination:

> I hate the damned country... To me it's not a question of choosing between poor old Dyer and the bloody browns. The choice was made for me when we took the country over and got the idea we did so far its own sake instead of ours. Dyer can look after himself, but according to the rules the browns can't because looking after them is what we get paid for.[27]

The characters of the Layton sisters - Sarah and Susan -are the real ones of the novel. The tragic past of the Laytons is narrated within the context of the events that took place between March and June, 1944. The British in India then had an acute sense of disaster since on March 18th the people of Pankot were startled by the news that the Japanese had crossed the Chindwin in force the day before. In this respect it can be said that the destinies of most of the characters are governed by the tragic force of history which is a significant aspect of Scott's historical imagination.

The character of Sarah is revealed through two incidents, first is the occasion when Sarah was taken by Ahmed for riding. However, in her attitude towards Indians she resembles Daphne Manners, who, though liberal in attitude, did maintain the idea of racial superiority in her personality. This is proved when Sarah maintained a distance between herself and Ahmed and thought that there was nothing to talk between them. Second was the 'incident of the stone'. When Teddie and Merrick were on their way to the palace guest house a stone was thrown at the car due to which Teddie was cut on the cheek. It was not known by whom the stone was thrown, though Pandit Baba was suspected to be behind it. The incident, indicative of the insecurity of the British arisen out of the Indian nationalist movement, was treated as 'childish and melodramatic' by Merrick.[28] However, this minor incident meant a lot to Sarah who described it as 'a vulgar anti-British demonstration'. It meant a lot to her because she thought owing to Indian vulgarity the British had achieved dignity. Her views are put in the following words:

> A stone: such a little thing. But look at us - Sarah thought - it has transformed us. We have acquired dignity. At no other time do we move with such grace as we do now when we feel threatened by violence but untouched by its vulgarity.[29]

Thus through the attitude of Sarah Scott is pointing out the moral uprightness of the British, which, no doubt, is Scott's point of view and therefore what Richard James thinks of Sarah is quite right:

> I think she was Paul Scott's favourite, and I think that it was through her that he cast his perceptive gaze on British India.[30]

The tragic fate of Susan makes Sarah comment on the British presence in India. In Sarah's opinion, the reason of Susan's tragedy was that the people like them were finished years ago and they knew it but pretended not to and went on as if they thought they still mattered. About this she says:

> So we hate each other, but daren't speak about it, and hate whatever lies nearest to hand, the country, the people in it, our own changing history that we are part of.[31]

Sarah's explanation why they are not important in the course of history underlines the British sense of frustration when she thinks:

> All India lies on our doorstep and cannot enter to warm us or be warmed. We live in holes and crevices of the crumbling stone, no longer sheltered by the carapace of our history which is leaving us behind. And one day we shall lie exposed, in our tender skins. You, as well as us.[32]

The other idea was the idea of security of the British in India. The British sense of insecurity is seen in Clark's views with whom she agrees. When Sarah visits him in Calcutta he says:

> This is the real Calcutta. I'm told this time last year these streets were littered with the corpses of people who came in to try and escape the famine. You have to hope that taxi doesn't conk out, they'd probably cut our throats and chuck us into the Hooghly.[33]

Here it must be seen that Scott is more concerned with the insecurity of the Britishers during the Bengal famine of war years than the sufferings of the Indians. How acute the problem of famine was can be gathered from Bhabani Bhattacharya's *So Many Hungers (1947)*. It is a story of the sufferings caused by the war and the consequent famine to the members of Kajoli's family in particular and to all the villagers of Bengal in general. Scott doesn't consider his moral responsibility to depict the effect of famine on humanity but finds expression in depicting the insecurity the British felt during that period.

The tragic effect of the novel is heightened by the character of Susan Layton because it is the effect of historical forces that govern her tragic fate. Her husband, Teddie Bingham, was killed in the war only a few months after their marriage. To intensify the effect, she is shown in the period of her first pregnancy. Scott has very touchingly depicted her sense of frustration caused by the untimely death of her husband. Her grief goes to the extent of killing her baby which we see in her talk. She says:

> At the service I prayed for the baby to die. I want him to die because I don't know how to face it alone. How can I face it with Teddie never coming back? I didn't want the baby, but it pleased him so, and I could face it like that. But I can't face it alone. I can't bear it alone.[34]

The Epilogue of the novel depicts the climax of the presentation of the tragic intensities faced by Susan. The climax is reached when Susan wants to put an end to her baby in the manner in which Dost Mohammed put the scorpion to death. Susan had in her mind the memory of the day of the scorpion, the day Dost Mohammed made a little circle of kerosene-soaked cotton waste, set light to it and then opened a circular tin, shook it, and dropped the small black scorpion into the centre of the ring of fire. When the flames died down the scorpion was dead. Similarly, Susan also wanted her child to die.

She, therefore, placed it on the grass, sprinkled a wide circle of Kerosene around it and set it to fire. But Minnie, the maid servant, snatched a sheet from the dhobi's bundle, ran and threw the sheet on to the flames, entered the circle and picked the child up and carried it to safety.[35] Benita Parry has aptly explained the meaning of this symbol. In her opinion, when the widowed Susan Bingham tries to kill her baby in a circle of flames her action reflects on the whole Anglo-Indian community, as if her madness were a larger statement about people doomed to suffer.[36] The symbol is further explained by Weinbaum:

> Parochial forces are the crushing enemies that are often and memorably symbolised in Scott's novels. Like the recurrent image of the scorpion the British Raj and the human condition are surrounded by indifferent and destructive forces.[37]

Here Scott implicitly believes that though the British Raj was progressive in outlook towards India the parochial forces of Indian nationalism brought it into the danger of extinction.

The characters of Sir George Malcom, Merrick - the same Merrick of *The Jewel* - and Teddie Bingham are revealed in the context of the contemporary political situation, Malcolm is presented as a pukka British officer. After Ex-Chief Minister MAK was arrested on August 9, 1942 under the Defence of India Rules there followed a meeting between him and Sir George Malcolm, the Governor of the province. The meeting is important since it throws light on Malcolm's belief that the British presence in India was necessary, because he felt that the Indians will not make proper rulers of India if the British withdraw from India. This view is clearly reflected in the following words:

> What did your people expect us to do? Sit back and let you bring the country to a standstill?[38]

The British policy of divide and rule is also to be noticed through his character. Throughout his talk with Kasim he is always making him conscious of his Muslim identity. For instance, he points out that since the Congress majority in the province was slim enough to warrant a coalition Mr Kasim wanted one Mr Nawaz Shah in his cabinet but none of his Congress colleagues would agree because he was a Muslim Leaguist. Further he describes the Congress party as a communal party and tries to implant the idea of division in Mr Kasim's mind. In this connection Malcolm says:

> You saw that whatever the Congress professed to be, a national party, a secular party, a party dedicated to the ideal of independence and national unity, there were people in it who could never see it as anything but a Hindu dominated organisation whose real motive was power for the Hindus and who were coming into the open now that they'd got power. That alarmed you too. Every instance that came to your notice of a Muslim being discriminated against, of an injustice against a Muslim, of violence done to a Muslim, of Muslim children being forced to salute the Congress flag or sing a Congress hymn in school.[39]

Scott believes that the British ideas were really progressive when Malcolm points out that by resigning the federal government the Congress has committed a folly. Malcolm also mentions that the Congress could have shown faith in the Cripps Mission, which again was a British idea. Scott's idea of paternalism is evident in Malcolm's speech when he believes that the British are going to save India from Japan. He says:

> You know the British simply aren't going to forgive all this Quit India nonsense going on while they're trying to concentrate on turning the tables on the Japanese, not - mark you - just to save themselves and their country but you and your country.[40]

Though Malcolm calls Quit India Movement a nonsense it has been treated as one of the major historical movements by most of the Indo-Anglian novelists. How effective the movement was can be seen in Bhabani Bhattacharya's *So Many Hungers* (1947) in which we can see the power of the movement in Rahoul's activities. It can be noticed in Rahoul's speech:

Quit India' cried the two million dead of Bengal. The anger was warm in his voice, and he had paused till his speech was cool again. 'Quit' cried all India. 'You have done us some good along with much evil. For the good you have done you have been paid in full. The accounts have been settled. Now for God's sake, quit.'[41]

Thus, by refusing to admit the significance of the Quit India Movement Scott has marginalised the historical fact of Indian nationalism. In the same manner, here also Scott distorts the image of Indian National Army and Gandhi.

Ronald Merrick, who was a police officer in *The Jewel*, reappears in this novel as a military officer. And it is through him that Scott has distorted the image of Gandhi. For instance, he thought that Gandhi's activities were nonsensical and believed that even the youngsters didn't believe in Gandhi and says:

They laugh at Gandhi, you know, all that crowd. All that passive resistance and nonviolence nonsense is just a joke to them, just as it's a joke to the militant Hindu wing of the Congress and organisations like the Mahasabha and the RSS.[42]

The fact that the death of Teddie involves the activities on Indian National Army founded by Subhas Chandra Bose makes the matter more serious. It was due to, according to the British, the treacherous act of the Indians that the INA was formed and it was the INA that killed Teddie. The very thing that the INA members were regarded as traitors establishes Scott's point of view as coloniser.

In Sarah's visit to Ronald Merrick who was admitted in the officers' wing of the military hospital of Calcutta explains how due to INA members Teddie had to lose his life. The INA members were known as Jiffs. They were the Indian soldiers who were once prisoners-of-war of the Japanese in Burma and Malaya, but later on they turned coat and formed themselves into army formations to help the enemy. There were a lot of them in the attempt the Japanese made to invade India through Imphal. Speaking about historical factuality we can say that Scott maintains it so far as the formation of INA is concerned but distorts the way in which it functioned. It did serve the cause of Indian national freedom which is criticised by Scott. Merrick feels very much sorry for the INA members' disloyalty shown to the British. It does mean that Scott thinks of the entire issue from the British point of view. The question of loyalty disturbs Merrick when he says:

> And officers like Teddie took it to heart. They couldn't believe Indian soldiers who'd eaten the King's salt and been proud to serve in the army generation after generation could be suborned like that, buy their way out of prison camp by turning coat, come armed hand in hand with the Japs to fight their own countrymen, fight the very officers who had trained them, cared for them and earned their respect.[43]

It means Merrick's attitude towards the INA is that of a British officer who did not want Indians to challenge the British rule in India.

Merrick explains in detail to Sarah how Teddie was killed. One Mr Mohammed Baksh of the INA was captured and Merrick fired questions at him and got a lot of information about the INA from him. In the course of the discussion Merrick frowns at Subhas Bose since he held him responsible for the opposition to the British and says:

> There'll be a day of reckoning I suppose. God knows what will happen to all those chaps. The strength of the INA is three divisions. That's a lot of officers and a lot of men. a lot of sentences of death. Too many. I suppose we might hang Subhas Chandra Bose, who's at the head of the whole thing.[44]

It is quite obvious that the image of Subhas Bose as a traitor is a distortion because Scott doesn't recognise him as an Indian national leader with moral force. In this connection Scott shows his interest in demonstrating the paternal attitude of the British. Even though Baksh had defected, Teddie felt compassion for him and said to him:

> You're still a soldier. Act like one. You've done very wrong, but I am still your father and mother.[45]

After Baksh was investigated there followed an attempt to find out Aziz Khan and Fariqua Khan, Baksha's companions involved in the plot in which

Teddie was killed when his jeep was overthrown in the bomb explosion on the track and in an attempt to save Teddie Merrick got wounded and lost one of his arms. In the entire INA story what Scott is preoccupied with is his serious concern with the moral integrity in the character of Teddie which is documented with profuse details. He has created the character of Teddie with full of physical and moral courage. His commitment to the job was that of an amateur. It was his commitment to the Raj value of paternalism because of which he has to lose his life. He says:

> Teddie and me, and why I say he died an amateur. He went down there for the regiment. I told you there was a touch of old-fashioned gallantry in it. All that paternalist business really meant something to him. Man-bap. I am your father and mother.[46]

Merrick means to say that though the attitude of paternalism was beneficial to the Indians they didn't recognise the worth of it. Thus, Scott considers that the idea of paternalism was progressive for the Indians. In Teddie's death he symbolises the death of Raj-values and feels deeply sorry for him. Merrick says to Sarah about this:

> Devotion, sacrifice, self-denial. A cause, an obligation. A code of conduct, a sort of final moral definition, I mean definition of us, what we're here for - people living among each other, in an environment some sort of God created.[47]

Merrick's views become so important that Sarah identifies herself with Merrick's grief and says that he was 'their dark side, the arcane side'. He revealed something sad about them, 'as if out there they had built a mansion without doors and windows, with no way in and no way out'.[48] Thus Merrick, who is treated as a critic of the ideals of the Raj in *The Jewel*, is regarded as a defender of the Raj-values in this volume.

Scott's depiction of the Congress-INA discord is historically quite true. This discord is revealed through the relationship between MAK, a staunch Congressman and Syed, his elder son, the member of the INA. It appears only in the last scene of the novel. The relationship is vital since in spite of their common aim - the expulsion of the British from India and achievement of self-rule - they were never in agreement with each other. In the last scene Mr Kasim meets his son Ahmed and his wife after his release from the Premanagar Fort. When he learns that his elder son Syed had joined the Indian National Army he immediately doesn't believe it because the very idea that his son would be fighting and killing Indians and helping the Japanese to invade his own country shocks him. His staunch belief in the ideals of Congress is proved once again when he expresses his anger against the INA in the following words:

> The Indian National Army? What can that be? A handful of madmen led by that other madman, Subhas Chandra Bose, who was never good to Congress. He always had delusions of grandeur.[49]

As far as the Congress-INA discord is concerned Scott is quite factual in his analysis, as the historian Michael Edwards observes: "Many Congressmen, including Mr Nehru were condemning Bose as a fascist. Indeed, he (Subhas Bose) had for some time been propounding a synthesis between fascism and communism".[50] This political idea was not acceptable to the Congress leaders who believed in the parliamentary democracy.. This discord in the context of the last days of the British Raj points out how Indians were not in agreement with each other and hence according to Scott, they were not mature to have a self-rule. Thus, as pointed out by the *Times Literary Supplement* reviewer, basically the novel is about 'the crumbling of an empire and about the changing attitudes discernible in those who - some of them for generations - have served it for as soldiers and administrators'.[51] Though the novel is about the "crumbling of an empire" Scott seems to ignore the nationalist feelings of the Indians.

NOTES AND REFERENCES

1   S.L. Hopkinson, review of *The Day of the Scorpion*, by Paul Scott, *Library Journal* (93: 3800), 15 October, 1968.

2   Keith Walker, 'Scott, Paul (Mark)", James Vinson (ed.), *Contemporary Novelists* (London: St. James Press, 1976), p. 1222.

3   R.H. Pearce, *Historicism Once More: Problems and Occasions for the American Scholar* (Princeton: Princeton Univ. Press, 1964), p. 6.

4   Paul Scott, *The Day of the Scorpion* (Frogmore: Panther Books, 1968), p. 11.

5   *Ibid.*, p. 9.

6   *Ibid.*, pp. 9-10.

7   Viscount Morley, quoted in Dennis Kincaid, *British Social Life in India, 1608-1937* (London: Routledge, 1938), p. 240.

8   Paul Scott, *The Day of the Scorpion* (Frogmore: Panther Books, 1968), p. 106.

9   *Ibid.*

10 *Ibid.*, p. 50.

11 *Ibid.*, p. 220.

12 *Ibid.*, p. 235.

13 *Ibid.*, p. 262.

14 *Ibid.*, p. 439.

15 *Ibid.*, p. 139.

16 *Ibid.*

17 *Ibid.*, p. 175.

18 *Ibid.*, p. 203.

19 *Ibid.*, p. 326.

20 *Ibid.*, p. 307.

21 Review of *The Day of the Scorpion*, by Paul Scott, *Times Literary Supplement*, 12 September 1968, p. 975.

22 Paul Scott, *The Day of the Scorpion* (Frogmore: Panther Books, 1968), p. 480.

23 Review of *The Day of the Scorpion*, by Paul Scott, *Times Literary Supplement*, 12 September, 1968, p. 975,

24 Paul Scott, *The Day of the Scorpion* (Frogmore: Panther Books, 1968), p. 108.

25 *Ibid.*, p. 109.

26 Patrick Swinden, *Paul Scott; Images of India* (London: Macmillan, 1980), p. 73.

27 Paul Scott, *The Day of the Scorpion* (Frogmore: Panther Books, 1968), p. 69.

28 *Ibid.*, p. 219.

29 *Ibid.*, p. 172.

30 Richard James, "In the Steps of Paul Scott," *The Listener*, 8 March, 1980, p. 359.

31 Paul Scott, *The Day of the Scorpion* (Frogmore: Panther Books, 1968), p. 354.

32 *Ibid.*, p. 4O9.

33 *Ibid.*, p. 431.

34 *Ibid.*, p. 342.

35 *Ibid.*, p. 494.

36 Benita Parry, "Paul Scott's Raj," *South Asian Review*, Vol. 8, No. 4, July, October, 1975, p. 363.

37 Francine Weinbaum, "Paul Scott's India: The Raj Quartet," *Critique*, 20:1 (197 9), p. 104.

38 Paul Scott, *The Day of the Scorpion* (Frogmore: Panther Books, 1968), p. 20.

39 *Ibid.*, pp. 21-22.

40 *Ibid.*, p. 24.

41 Bhabani Bhattacharya, *So Many Hungers* (Bombay: Hind Kitabs, 1947), pp. 212-213.

42 Paul Scott, *The Day of the Scorpion* (Frogmore: Panther Books, 19681, p. 207.

43 *Ibid.*, p. 385.

44 *Ibid.*, p. 395.

45 *Ibid.*, p. 398.

46 *Ibid.*, p. 404.

47 *Ibid.*, p. 408.

48 *Ibid.*, p. 409.

49 *Ibid.*, p. 479.

50 Michael Edwardes, *Raj* (Pan Books: 1969), p. 333.

51 Review of *The Day of the Scorpion*, by Paul Scott, *Times Literary Supplement*, 12 September 1968, p. 975.

3. *The Towers of Silence*

The Towers of Silence (1971)

In *The Towers of Silence* (1971), the third and penultimate volume of *The Raj Quartet*, Scott has recreated the British Indian history against the background of the turbulent situation that arose during the last days of the Raj mainly through the characters of Miss Barbara Batchelor, popularly known as Barbie, retired from her post as Superintendent of the Protestant mission schools in the city of Ranpur, and widowed Mrs Mabel Layton, Lieutnent Colonel John Layton's stepmother who was staying at Rose Cottage, a large rectangular structure built in the Anglo-Indian style which is elaborately described in the preceding volume, *The Day of the Scorpion*. The third volume continues Scott's idea of the importance of the British Raj values which he considers as progressive and creates an illusion of the moral aspect of the British presence in India, but with a slight difference. Unlike the previous two volumes, he does not concentrate on the Indian scene and Indian characters here but makes the sufferings of the British as his main concern and maintains the tragic atmosphere throughout the novel and hence what the *Times Literary Supplement* reviewer says is quite succinct:

> The tragic intensities of the British predicament in India makes the novel an elegy on the decline and fall of the Indian empire which sounds harsh notes.[1]

The fictitious characters of Barbie, Mabel and Mildred Layton as presented against the actual historical happenings give a definite dimension to Scott's historical imagination. As Doris Marston observes:

> It is legitimate to create your own characters and set them into a period of history, using exciting events as part of their lives.[2]

The period Scott deals with is undoubtedly of turbulent nature. At the turn of the year (1942) the war was on India's doorstep. The British lost Malaya, Singapore and Burma to the Japanese. Indian leaders thought that the British defeat in Malaya and Burma was a forerunner to defeat in India and that the British had shown themselves incompetent to defend India. The political situation was sizzling dangerously from the March of 1942, and finally exploded in August with a violence that set people talking about a new mutiny. Scott has maintained historical accuracy in giving these details. We will examine how he has created the British characters against this background. The very act of the circulation of this picture of 'The Jewel in the Crown' - a coloured engraving showing Queen Victoria receiving tribute from representatives of her Indian empire[3] - among the British indicates their belief in the values represented by that picture. Barbie, Edwina's successor, was also presented with the replica of the same picture. The picture is explained in relation to the personality of Teddie Bingham. When Sarah mentions this to Barbie she expresses her feelings which throw light on the paternalistic value of the Raj:

> Man-bap. She had not heard that expression for a long time. It meant Mother-Father, the relationship of the raj to India, of a man like Colonel Layton to the men in his regiment, of a district officer to the people of his district, of Barbie herself to the children she had taught. Man-bap. I am your father and mother. Yes, the picture had been an illustration of this aspect of the imperial attachment.[4]

Thus the recurrent image of paternalism, which, for Scott, is the part of the progressive nature of the Raj, helps to explain the characters created by him.

As far as the characters are concerned most of them are the same characters that appeared in *The Day of the Scorpion* and therefore the novel can be treated just as an appendage to it. The first important character is Barbara Batchelor. At the very beginning of the novel we learn that Barbie, who believed in the good will and good sense of established authority, had a basic role of Christian missionary in India which is evident when the author says, 'to Barbie, the teaching of reading, writing and arithmetic had never been as important as the teaching of Christianity'.[5] Her missionary zeal can be further noticed in the following words:

> To bring even one Hindu or Muslim child to God struck her as a very satisfactory thing to do and she imagined that in the mission it would be open to her to do this for scores, possibly hundreds.[6]

At this moment it is also interesting to note the British policy of education in India. Barbie's disappointment to find that instead of Christianity all the emphasis was upon the mission's educational function makes it necessary to discuss the British education policy. That the British administrators were not keen on Christian missionary element was a part of their colonial policy to keep their power intact in India - the policy which had its roots in the historical mutiny of 1857, 'which people said started because the Indian sepoys believed they were to be forcibly converted, having first been polluted by the introduction of cartridges greased with pig fat. The authorities, both civil and military, seemed to take considerable trouble to enable Hindus to go on being Hindus and Muslims to be Muslims by giving them every opportunity to practice their rites and hold their festivals and by giving official recognition to the communal differences between them'.[7] In this way in underlining the historical reason as to why the Christian element was not stressed in the school points to the British colonial policy.

Barbie's response to the violent attacks on Miss Crane and Miss Manners is meaningful. When she thinks of Daphne Manners she becomes critical of Indians. She believes that the violence done to Daphne was not over yet. She thought that when she will be taken to the court of law she will be psychologically harassed by the Indian lawyers pleading for the six Indian youths arrested in the Bibighar Gardens case. It is quite clear in Barbie's words:

> And the arrested men would not lack clever Bengali lawyers
> who would plead without fee, anxious for the publicity and
> the opportunity to sling mud, to impugn the morals of an
> English girl.[8]

These views correspond with Scott's basic idea of Indians as uncivilized people *vis-à-vis* British as superior ones. Barbie's response to the attack on Miss Crane is yet more significant since it highlights her staunch belief in essentially Christian missionary values as that of Miss Crane's. She always identifies herself with Miss Crane whose missionary work had remained incomplete. Thus the retelling of the entire story of Miss Crane is illuminating in so far as Barbie's role in British India is concerned. It also indicates, as pointed out by Martin Levin, that 'Barbie Batchelor has resigned her missionary calling but not her dedication to duty, sacrifice and selflessness which leads to some deeper relationships than are common in protocol-conscious enclave'.[9] Her human consideration is noted when she considers Daphne's child as one of God's creatures having heavenly scent. This is symbolically presented by Scott. He uses the symbol of the poems of Gaffur. She likes the poet because he describes the rose as God's creation and its scent heavenly. To quote the poem itself:

> It is not for you to say, Gaffur,
> That the rose is one of God's creations,
> Although its scent is doubtless that of heaven.
> In time rose and poet will both die.
> Who then shall come to this decision?
> (Trans. Edwin Tippit (Major I.A. Retd.)
> You oughtn't to say Gaffur,
> That God created Roses,
> No matter how heavenly they smell.
> You have to think of the time when
> you're both dead and smell and nasty
> And people are only interested in your successors
> (Trans. Dmitri Bronowsky).[10]

The poem is treated as symbolic by Barbie - symbolic of Daphne Manners' experience in India. Daphne is gone but her child, which she considers as God's creation, has left behind the heavenly scent. In a way, she also means to say that though Daphne is no more now she remained successful in establishing sort of rapport with the Indians. She is gone but she left something behind by which she is remembered. In the same way, Barbie thinks that even if the British leave India they will be remembered by their civilizing mission in India which has got a heavenly scent. So, at the base of the symbolic treatment of the poem of Gaffur there lies Scott's attitude towards India - India that is 'full of oddities'[11] and deadly requires civilizing mission by which the British will be remembered, Due to the backwardness of India how difficult it was for the British to teach the Indians is illustrated in a story of one of Barbie's friends who belonged to what was called a zenana mission. Her job was to try to give the rudiments of a modern education to the rulers' wives and daughters who were all in purdah or going to be in purdah. 'She adored the children but said there were times when she actually went in fear of her life, not that it was ever threatened but she heard some terrible things, quite barbaric.[12] This image of Indians as backward is quite similar to that depicted in *The jewel*.

She does not like the people who neglected the Raj-values and feels deeply sorry for the people like Mabel Layton who represented the Raj in the true sense of the term. And, therefore, the death of Mabel is symbolic to her. It symbolises for her the death of the Raj itself. Hence she thinks at the time of Mabel's burial:

> There went the raj, supported by the unassailable criteria of necessity, devoutness, even of self-sacrifice.[13]

She believes that since the people like Mildred did not believe in the dignity of the Raj they were responsible to lose it. She further believes that it was the British intention to civilise the Indians as long as the Raj was there. But, unfortunately, they couldn't complete their mission due to the end of the Raj - the end, to some extent, according to Scott, was the result of the negligence of the Raj-values on the part of the people like Mildred. Though disappointed with people like Mildred, she makes her stand clear in the following words:

> And it will be (Barbie thought) so it will be in regard to our experience here. And when we are gone let them colour the sky how they will, we shall not care. It has never truly been our desire or intention to colour it permanently but only to make it as cloudless for ourselves as we can.[14]

In these words Scott tries to show how strongly Barbie is conscious of the British integrity and moral uprightness. The author is not worried in the way the Indians will run their country but he is worried about their position as long as they remain in India.

Barbie's tragedy begins when, after Mabel's death, she was given an official notice to leave the Rose Cottage and was in difficulty to find out an accommodation. In this context, Scott is critical of Mildred Layton who was the cause of Barbie's tragedy. He means to say that it was because of the Mildreds - heavily addicted to drinks and satisfying their sexual thirst by commiting adultery - that the Barbies had to suffer - the Barbies, who, by their devout nature, served the Raj. Thus, as pointed out by Weinbaum, Barbie is the novel's 'most explicit and sustained symbol of the British in India.'[15] Scott identifies the British Raj with Barbie and when she is rendered homeless he points out:

> A comic but horrifying thought took place: of old Miss Batchelor, homeless, seated on a trunk in the middle of the

bazaar, surrounded by her -detritus, unpacking and rebuilding the. monument there, to the amusement of Hindu and Muslim shopkeepers who would interpret such a sight as proof that the entire raj would presently and similarly be on its uppers.[16]

Thus, as pointed out by the *Times Literary Supplement* reviewer, in Barbie, we are provided with an example of the disintegrating character brought about by the manner in which a personality in many ways distinguished, and certainly distinctive, is affected by the Indian experience.[17]

Barbie's leaving the Rose Cottage is also given symbolic treatment. It symbolises the British withdrawal from India. At the time of her departure from the Rose Cottage Barbie collects the roses from the bushes and says to them:

'You are now native roses', she said to them. Of the country. The garden is a native garden. We are only-visitors. That has been our mistake. That is why god has not followed us here.[18]

Symbolically, the garden is India and the roses in it are Indians, as the gardener takes care of his garden, Scott implicitly says, the British took care of the Indians. However, their work is incomplete and Barbie, therefore, is unhappy to leave India. The symbol also points out Barbie's paternalistic attitude towards Indians. It means Barbie strongly feels that Indians are not yet well civilized. This view is illustrated when Barbie was provided with an alternative accommodation at Clarissa Peplow's. She faced the problem of the storage of her luggage which couldn't be accommodated in a small room given to her. Clarissa, therefore, suggests her to speak at Jalal-Ud-Din's who had some facilities about the storage. Barbie didn't welcome the idea and said, "That won't be necessary, Clarissa. I should not want my stuff mouldering in a native storehouse."[19] This obviously brings to our mind that in spite of her high ideals of missionary work, she does not show a simple belief in the Indians. She further thought that she should not be happy to think of her trunk in a 'heathen store-room' and believed that the trunk was packed with relics of her work in the mission. She treated it as her life in India.[20] The symbol of the trunk is used to show the British sense of history. In this connection she says to Sarah:

The trunk is a very different kettle of fish. Unlike a writing-table, unlike one's clothes, one's shoes, it is of no use. But it

is my history. And according to Emerson without it, without
that, I'm simply not explained. I am a body, sitting here.
Without it, according to Emerson, none of us is explained
because if it is my history then it is your too and was Mabel's.[21]

Scott's preoccupation with history is noted here since he believes that
individual lives are inseparable from the process of history and British people
can be better explained in the context of the British Raj and therefore it forms
an important aspect of Scott's historical imagination.

Barbie's paternal attitude towards Indians becomes clear from the following
dialogue between her and Ashok, an orphan Indian boy of eight years:

> 'What am I?' She asked Ashok.
> You are Sahib-log'.
> No, I am a servant of the Lord Jesus.'
> She sat on the verandah steps of the rectory bungalow and
> offered her hand. Ashok looked at her seriously. 'Come', she
> said, 'I am your father and your mother.'[22]

Here Scott reveals how the British were committed to their ideals.

The last scene of the novel brings out, quite effectively in a symbolic
manner, how the British responded to the demise of the British Raj. At the end
we learn that Barbie is hospitalised as she has got brancho-pneumonia and she
is under a vow of silence. Once she points through the barred window and asks
Sister Mary Thomas More, in writing, the meaning of the birds, the vultures,
beyond the minaret. The sister replies that the birds are the carrion birds which
belong to the towers of silence, for the Ranpur Parsees. Barbie's incorrigible
state of mind is important since she often sat at the window watching through
narrowed hungry eyes the birds that fed on the dead bodies of the Parsees.[23]
The symbol means that the dead bodies are nothing but the end of the British
Raj in India and the vultures encircling on the tower mean the Indian national
leaders expecting the self-rule in India. The symbol of vultures used for the
Indians indicates that they are greedy persons profiting from the misfortunes of
the British. This is a total distortion of the image of Indian leaders. In this way,
the character of Barbie becomes 'the presiding genius of *The Towers of Silence*.'[24]

One can read the history of British in India in the person of Mrs Mabel
Layton who was living a lonely sort of life at Rose Cottage in Pankot. In Rose

Cottage there were photographs of Laytons, and of Mabel's first husband and his family and all of them, looked distinguished and well off, very pukka, the kind of people who belonged to the ruling class in India. Scott is interested in pointing out the pukka trait in Mabel's personality which can be seen in Scott's analysis of her:

> Mabel, it was true, had let herself go, but in the manner that only people of her upbringing seemed capable of doing without losing prestige and an air of authority.[25]

Mabel's connection with British Indian history is very close is seen in the fact that 'she was herself what Anglo-Indian society called Army: Army by her first husband, Civil by her second and Army again by her second husband's son, her stepson, no less a person than the commanding officer of the 1st Pankot Rifles which Barbie had heard enough about to know was a very distinguished regiment indeed, particularly in the eyes of the Pankot people.[26] Scott is pointing out the pukka element in the British only to establish his racial outlook towards history.

All the while Scott is drawing our attention to Mabel's recluse life which has got its roots in British Indian history. Mabel's background was impeccable. Her absorption in garden and bungalow, her habit of taking solitary walks, her refusal even of invitations it was generally considered obligatory to accept, her complete detachment from Pankot public life, are attributed to the personal idiosyncrasy of someone who has lost two husbands in the cause of service to the empire, one by rifle fire on the Kyber, the other by amoebic infection.[27] Scott says that Mabel's personal loss which caused her withdrawal, is rooted in the British Indian history and thus consolidates his idea that individuals are better explained in the context of their history. Scott's feeling of reverence for the golden age which everyone knew had gone but over whose memory she stood 'guardian, stony-faced and uncompromising'.[28] Moreover, Scott has given a symbolic treatment to the story of Mabel, 'a doyenne of the army cast superstructure at the hill-station of Pankot,[29] which, he believes, is the story of the glorious days of the Raj which is no more and which gives the notice of unpleasant consequences British might face with in India. He says:

> a bleak point of reference, as it were a marker-buoy above a sunken ship full of treasure that could never be salvaged; a

reminder and a warning to shipping still afloat in waters that
got more treaturous every year.[30]

Here the sunken ship means the British Raj at its end which was full of
good things, an inexhaustible treasure of good values which were at stake due
to the treaturous waters which mean the growing unrest in India. The symbol
again speaks of the grandeur of the British Raj and points out Scott's British
outlook.

The death of Mabel, is again given a symbolic treatment by Scott. It is
intended to mean the end of the Raj. It is illustrated with a metaphor in the
following lines:

> It drew attention to a situation it was painful to acknowledge:
> that the god had left the temple, no one knew, when, or how,
> or why. What one was left with were rites which had once
> propitiated, once been obligatory, but now were meaningless
> because the god was no longer there to receive them.[31]

The god here is the British Raj crystalised in the values cherished by the
people like Mabel Layton. But her death brought meaninglessness to the Raj
because the people like Mildred Layton didn't care for the values of the Raj.

The christening shawl possessed by Mabel also brings out the symbolism
of the British in India. The story behind the shawl is that it was made by an
old retainer of Mabel's French mother-in-law (by her first husband). The old
lady lived in the tower of Chateau in the lie de France. When Mabel visited her
many years ago, and received the present of the lace shawl, she saw that on it
was a motif of butterflies: 'They were alive, fluttering above her moving hand.'
And the old lace-maker answered that 'her heart bled for the butterflies because
they could never fly out of the prison of the lace and make love in the sunshine.
She could feel the sunshine on her hands but her hands were nothing but a
prison for God's most delicate creatures.'[32] How this delicate and suggestive
story is related to the Raj is pointed out by Patrick Swinden. He believes, that
one can see the application of the story to the position of the British in India.
And one takes note of psychological comparisons between the blind old lady,
creating beauty out of a simulated death; and several of the characters in the
novel, who blindly imprison their most urgent desires in a cage of memory or
fantasy or a vacuous simulacrum of the satisfactions to which they aspired'.[33]

That the behaviour of Scott's characters is closely linked with the effects of historical situations is once again proved in case of Mildred Layton, Lt. Colonel John Layton's wife. The cause of her compulsive drinking habit lies in a shocking news to her - the news in 1941 that the 1st Pankots had been severely mauled in North Africa and Colonel Layton with the remnants of his command taken prisoner by the Italians.[34] Mildred was getting just a half colonel's pay that did not support the style of life which she was accustomed to and which she kept up rather better than anyone else. And therefore the author says that it was ironic to think that so much of raj's elegance which provoked the Indian temper had always been supported by private incomes.[35] In this context he points out the virtuous nature of the British people. In his opinion, 'from Viceroy down the difference between his pay and allowances and necessary expenses meant that a man was usually out of pocket administering or defending the empire. One was used to debt, to cutting down; to the sense of imminent shabiness in approaching retirement.[36] This view of Scott does speak of the commitment the British had to their assigned work.

Scott recurrently points out the tragic aspect of Mildred Layton as a lady of virtue - 'the virtue that attached to her as Colonel Layton's wife was crystallized by the other virtues of her family connection with the station'[37] - who had been abandoned to cope alone with the problems of a way of life which was under attack from every quarter but in which she had no 'honourable course' but to continue. Her strong commitment to her duty is recorded in the following words:.

> Mildred's enemy was history not an early death in exile, but neither end was the kind that could have been or could be assumed, and the evidence of cessation which a clear look into the future might reveal did not countermand her duty to the existing order of things if she continued to believe in it.[38]

Scott's strength lies in the fact that though he appreciates Mildred's virtues he criticises her when she indulges in drinking and sexual foibles resulting into the neglegence of the Raj-values on her part. For example, she gives so much importance to the so-called prestige of the British that she doesn't recognise the human element in Daphne Manners' decision of giving birth to her child instead of the advice of abortion. She (Mildred) says:

> The girl, the Manners girl (poor running panting Daphne)
> had paid the price of her folly by dying, bearing the tiny
> monster of the Bibighar that should have been destroyed in
> the womb.[39]

These views, which are totally opposite of Barbie's who believed the child as God's creation, certainly expose the character of Mildred as inhuman.

Mildred's contemptuous attitude towards Barbie also reflects on her personality. It is revealed when she did not display the twelve Apostle Silver spoons given by Barbie to Susan as a gift at the time of wedding reception and later returned the spoons to her. Besides this humiliating treatment given to Barbie there is one more occasion which reveals Mildred's attitude. Once Mabel had expressed her wish to Barbie that after her demise she should be buried in the Churchyard of St Luke's in Ranpur near her second husband. But after her death Mildred had arranged the interment at St. John's Churchyard. So, when Barbie went to Mildred to remind her of this, Mildred insulted her by calling her "bloody bitch"[40] and asked her to leave the place. This attitude of Mildred, Barbie believed, was not in keeping with the Raj-values which were cherished by the people like Mabel Layton. Thus in the criticism of the character of Mildred, like that of Ronald Merrick in *The Jewel in the Crown*, Scott expresses his indignation towards the British who neglected the Raj-values.

As far as Scott's minor characters are concerned, he delineates them, as affected by the historical forces and in doing so he illustrates one of the important features of the historical novel as pointed out by Fleishman who thinks:

> The historical novel is pre-eminently suited to telling how
> individual lives were shaped at specific moments of history,
> and how this shaping reveals the character of those historical
> periods.[41]

For example, we are informed that Colonel Paynton of the Ranpurs has been killed in the Arakan and Nicky, his widowed wife, is packing up and going home by the quickest means available. How the very existence of the British in India was conditioned by the major historical forces is shown in the departure of Nicky Paynton:

With one stroke India was finished for her and although she would probably assure her friends that she'd be back, this was one of those crystal clear cases of a woman leaving and knowing that her chances of seeing India again were slim enough to be non-existent.[42]

If we compare the image of an Englishwoman during this period of turbulance with that of John Masters', his contemporary, we get convinced of Scott's attitude. For example, in *Bugles and a Tiger; A Volume of Autobiography*, Masters gives a detailed picture of a memsahib. Prof. Shamsul Islam's comment sums up the description of a memsahib as depicted by Masters. He writes:

> The memsahib had. her scores of servants to tend to every chore, and thus she had nothing much to do except indulge in socialising, scandal-mongering, or internal feuds. However, life in India was not a bed of roses even for a memsahib. Details of material comfort varied and then there was always the danger of disease: rabies, typhoid, smallpox and cholera rampant; snakes, mosquitoes, and scorpions abundant; and sunstroke common.[43]

The difference in approach can very easily be noticed here. Though Masters depicts the memsahib of the same period which Scott deals with, he totally neglects the effect of historical forces on the memsahib.

As far as Scott's consideration of the working of All India Congress, Indian National Army and views of Gandhi are concerned it is to be seen that he denounces them as seen in the earlier volumes. For example, he calls Gandhi an insensible person and 'Quit India' movement funny one. He says:

> His demand now the British should quit India, should leave her to 'God or to anarchy' sounded fine, courageous, desparate and inspired, but it meant that they should leave India to the Japanese who were already on the Chindwin but with whom Gandhi obviously expected to make a political bargain. Unless you were stupid you did not make bargains with the Japanese but war.[44]

Scott's harsh criticism of INA is again seen in one of the conversations between Mrs Paynton and Mrs Fosdick, the wives of the British officers in India:

> If ever we do win this bloody war we might hang Bose and one or two bigwigs but the rest will just have to be cashiered or dismissed with ignominy. Only by then we'll probably be on our way out in any case and the bloody Indians will have to deal with them in their own bloody way, and they'll probably bloody well make heroes out of them.[45]

We can conclude that though Scott maintains historical facts his point of view remains the same (as seen in the earlier volumes) in his criticism of the INA and Gandhi.

Since the novel does not disengage itself from some of the events in the preceding two volumes, for instance, Teddie Bingham's marriage with Susan Layton and his tragic end, appearance of Miss Manners and Gandhi, etc, it is criticised as repetitious and having only about one fourth material that is new.[46] However, in the opinion of John Skow, part of the justification for retelling all this is 'Scott's representation of three exceptional women characters - Mabel, Mildred and Barbie'.[47] It is quite acceptable because their personalities are developed in a full-fledged manner against the background of the preceding volumes and hence repetitiousness becomes inevitable.

NOTES AND REFERENCES

1   Review of *The Towers of Silence*, by Paul Scott, *Times Literary Supplement*, 10 October, 1971, p. 1199.

2   Doris Marston, *A Guide to Writing History* (Cincinnati OH 45242: Writer Digest Division, F & W Publishing Corporation, 1976), p. 104.

3   Paul Scott, *The Towers of Silence* (Frogmore: Panther Books, 1971), p. 25.

4   *Ibid.*, p. 275.

5   *Ibid.*, p. 10.

6   *Ibid.*, pp. 10-11.

7   *Ibid.*, p. 11.

8   *Ibid.*, p. 68.

9   Martin Levin, rev. of *The Towers of Silence* by Paul Scott, *The New York Times Book Review*, 20 February, 1972, p. 26.

10 Paul Scott, *The Towers of Silence* (Frogmore: Panther Books, 1971), p. 174.

11 *Ibid*, p. 176.

12 *Ibid.*

13 *Ibid.*, p. 245.

14 *Ibid.*

15 Francine Weinbaum, "Paul Scott's India; *The Raj Quartet*," *Critique* (20:1) 1979,- p. 107.

16 Paul Scott, *The Towers of Silence* (Frogmore: Panther Books, 1971), p. 259.

17 Review of *The Towers of Silence* by Paul Scott, *Times Literary Supplement*, 10 October 1971, p. 1199.

18 Paul Scott, *The Towers of Silence* (Frogmore: Panther Books, 1971), p. 283.

19 *Ibid.*, p. 267.

20 *Ibid.,* p. 280.

21 *Ibid.*, pp. 279-80.

22 *Ibid.*, p. 364.

23 *Ibid.*, p. 396.

24 Review of *The Towers of Silence* by Paul Scott, *Times Literary Supplement*, 10 October 1971, p. 1199.

25 Paul Scott, *The Towers of Silence* (Frogmore: Panther Books, 1971), p. 20.

26 *Ibid.*, p. 22.

27 *Ibid.,* p. 32.

28 *Ibid.*

29　Review of *The Towers of Silence* by Paul Scott, *Times Literary Supplement*, 10 October 1971, p. 1199.

30　Paul Scott, *The Towers of Silence* (Frogmore: Panther Books, 1971), p. 32.

31　*Ibid.,* pp. 261-62.

32　*Ibid.*, p. 188.

33　Patrick Swinden, *Paul Scott; Images of India* (London: Macmillan, 1980), p. 100.

34　Paul Scott, *The Towers of Silence* (Frogmore: Panther Books, 1971), p. 42.

35　*Ibid.*, p. 45.

36　*Ibid.*

37　*Ibid.*

38　*Ibid.*, p. 46. -

39　*Ibid.,* p. 171.

40　*Ibid.*, p. 241.

41　Avrom Fleishman, *The English Historical Novel; Walter Scott to Virginia Woolf* (Baltimore & London: Johns Hopkins Press, 1971), p. 10.

42　Paul Scott, *The Towers of Silence* (Frogmore: Panther Books, 1971), p. 311.

43　Shamsul Islam, *Chronicles of the Raj; A study of Literary Reaction to the Imperial Idea towards the End of the Raj* (London: Macmillan, 1979), p. 88.

44　Paul Scott, *The Towers of Silence* (Frogmore: Panther Books, 1971), p. 5o.

45　*Ibid.*, pp. 254-55.

46　Review of *The Towers of Silence* by Paul Scott, *Choice,* July, August, 1972, 9:647.

47　John Skow, rev. of *The Towers of Silence* by Paul Scott, *Time,* March 27, 1972.

4. *A Division of the Spoils*

A Division of the Spoils (1975)

A Division of the Spoils (1975), the fourth and concluding volume of *The Raj Quartet*, recreates the British Indian history, especially of the years between 1945 and 1947. In continuation with the preceding three volumes it reveals Scott's British position on the Raj. He believes that due to the rift between Muslims and Hindus India shouldn't be given freedom so early. But it didn't happen so and the Indians achieved their freedom which resulted in the violence between the two communities. These views are clearly expressed by Scott in the following words;

> The political impasse between Muslims and Hindus during the negotiations for British withdrawal and the bloody events that accompanied the birth of the two new independent dominions of India and Pakistan, seemed to prove that the Raj was right all along.[1]

This idea leads us to consider Scott's belief that the Raj held the balance of power between otherwise irreconcilable forces that would lose no opportunity to cheat, to threaten or slaughter one another and the Raj restricted this in the sense that it imposed a single rule of law upon all its people.[2]

As pointed out by Webster Schott, some of the characters and stories from the previous novel are remembered, repeated and seen in other colours by Scott's characters in this novel.[3] However, there is an introduction of a new important character, Guy Perron, a Sergeant in Field Security and a student of British Indian history who seems to be a mouthpiece of the author. The activities of Nigel Rowan, now an ADC to the Provincial Governor, are also important in the development of the plot. Ronald Merrick, whose face is disfigured and who has got a mechanical arm is also seen again. He later on gets married to Susan and is killed by certain people during the last days of the Raj. Bronowsky is seen planning to create a new political order in Mirat by marrying Shiraz, the Nawab's only daughter, to Ahmed, MAK's son. And there is the final tragedy in the train from Mirat to Ranpur in which the conflict between the races becomes uncontrollable in which Ahmed is killed. There are some other important happenings in the novel too - Colonel Layton's returning to Pankot, Sarah's attachment with Perron and the functioning of the operation Zipper.

In the context of this fictitious background Scott has presented the real historical happenings which are, in the words of Schott, as follows: 'the sweeping events in Scott's novel are enormous social dislocations caused by World War II and British ambiguity and repression in response to Indian agitation for independence. Moving back and forth, from a distance to the foreground, are the raj's imprisonment of Indian politicians, the refusal of Indian leaders to support the war effort, British defeat by the Japanese in Burma, the organization of an Indian National Army (composed of Japan's Indian prisoners) to liberate India from British rule, the jokeying for position among Hindus, Moslems and vassal princes as the collapse of the raj draws near and partitioning of India appears inevitable'.[4] Thus, a complete fusion of fact and fiction makes the novel an interesting historical novel. It is also seen in case of the use of characters. Besides the use of fictitious characters like Perron, Merrick, Sarah and others he also uses the characters of Gandhi, Nehru, Wavell and others. In doing so Scott illustrates Fleishman's view regarding the historical novel:

> The historical novel is distinguished among novels by the presence of a specific link to history: not merely a real building or a real event but a real person among the fictitious ones.[5]

It is to be seen that Scott meticulously maintains the chronological order of the historical events and accommodates them very skilfully in the narrative structure of the novel. The historical events are not merely external things grafted on the main story; they are the organic parts of the story.

Perron becomes the key-character of the novel because in one of his notes he reflects Scott's views regarding the British Raj mentioned at the very beginning of this chapter. Perron writes:

> For at least a hundred years India has formed part of England's idea about herself and for the same period India has been forced into a position of being a reflection of that idea. Up to say 1900 the part India played in our idea about ourselves was the part played by anything we possessed which we believed it was right to possess (like a special relationship with God).[6]

It was only at the beginning of twentieth century that Indians became active in respect of their nationalism the fact that is not appreciated by Perron.

Hence he says that only before 1900 India reflected their ideas. He believes that after 1900, certainly since 1918, the reverse had happened. The part played since then by India in the English idea of Englishness had been that of something they felt it did them no credit to have. Their idea about themselves would not accommodate any idea about India except the idea of returning it to the Indians in order to prove that they were English and had demonstrably English ideas.[7] It means that India was granted independence not because of the external pressure of nationalism, etc, but because of the internal pressure which is seen in the belief that the Indians have lost faith in the English idea. Such a strong belief in English ideas as shown by Scott points out his respect for Englishness. Hence Perron becomes very much aware of his identity as the British. His exclusive belief in the British ideas is recorded by him in the following words:

> All this is quite simply proven and amply demonstrated. But on either side of that arbitrary date (1900) India itself, as itself, that is to say India as not part of our idea of ourselves, has played no part whatsoever in the lives of Englishmen in general (no part that we are conscious of) and those who came out (those for whom India had to play a real part) became detached both from English life and from English idea of life. Getting rid of India will cause us at home no qualm of conscience because it will be like getting rid of what is no longer reflected in our mirror of ourselves. The sad thing is that whereas in the English mirror there is now no India-reflection (think of Purvis, those men I lectured to, and the corporal here in the guardroom), in the Indian mirror of the English reflection may be very hard to get rid of, because in the Indian mind English possession has not been idea but a reality; often a harsh one.[8]

The expression that the British will not get disturbed by their conscience in granting freedom to India because India had ceased to believe in their ideas which was the basis of the Raj in India speaks of the Britishers' staunch belief in their ideas regarding the Raj. It also tells how powerfully Scott makes his characters imbibe these ideas, which, Patrick Swinden thinks, is the reason why Scott's account rings true. He writes:

The reason this account rings true to anyone reading it in its proper setting in *The Quartet* is that the beliefs and ideas it talks about have been fully dramatised in the lives of many of the characters we have met.[9]

Scott's belief in paternalism, one of the British ideas, is illustrated through the history of Indian princes at the end of the Raj. In one of the conversations between Rowan and Bronowsky Scott has revived the history of the princely states by taking the example of the State of Mirat. Bronowsky, who confidently believes that he would not have political or communal disturbances stirred up in Mirat, defends the princes' ability to rule the states properly. His apathy for the Indian national movement of Independence becomes obvious when he takes the major Indian political parties responsible for attempting communal riots in the past twenty years. Again his belief in the ability of the princes is proved when he says that in spite of Nawab's being a Muslim and the majority of his subjects Hindu the two communities had equal opportunities and were content as his subjects. This contentment is evident, Bronowsky believes, in their not being attracted by the new patriotic consciousness created by Mahatma Gandhi. In case of Mirat's subjects he says:

> (they) do not hanker after the democratic millenium promised by Gandhiji on the one hand or the theistic paradise-state on earth envisaged by Jinnah on the other.[10]

it means that the princes were interested in retaining their states which is historically quite true. However, when the British, their parents, are left there will not be any autocratic future for the states. This becomes obvious in the following lines:

> ... when the British finally go. No freedom separate from India's freedom. No separate future for Mirat nor for any of the states, with the possible exception of the largest and most powerful such as Hyderabad....[11]

Scott means to say that the princes will be rendered helpless after the departure of the British, the view that conforms to his idea of paternalism.

Scott maintains historical fidelity when he believes that the princes thought that they would be in difficulty after the transfer of power which is reflected in Nawab's attitude towards the British and Gandhi and Nehru. The Nawab of Mirat thought that since they had supplied the British with money and men in the two world wars the British were pledged to protect their rights and their privileges and their authority. However, they could not have a treaty with the British since it won't be valid after their departure. It would be just a piece of paper. A new treaty will have to be made with the people who had taken over from the British. The princes will have to negotiate a new treaty with Mr Gandhi and Mr Nehru but which was impossible because of the Congress' faith in democracy. It is revived through the views of MAK, representing the Congress, and the views of Bronowsky, representing the views of the states. That the Congress was not for the existence of the states is explicit in the following statement of MAK:

> Count Bronowsky and I don't have any intimate relationship,
> in spite of my younger son's connection with him. He and
> I are politically opposed. He is dedicated to the continuing
> autocratic authority of the Nawab. I am dedicated to the
> diminution and final extinction of the autocratic authority of
> all the Indian Princes.[12]

Thus, India will face the problem of the princes after independence. And apart from that India will be facing the most severe problem of communalism and separatism. Here Scott doubts the ability of the Indians to tackle these problems and hence believes in the value of the Raj which was administering the things quite smoothly.

The communal spirit between the Hindus and the Muslims which resulted in the separatist tendency is given importance by Scott in the event of the Indian independence. First it is revealed through the story of MAK. 'In 1937, MAK had not included Hamidullah Khan, a staunch Congressman who had defeated a Muslim Leaguist, in the ministry but later on regretted not having given the old man his chance since he thought a Muslim minister for education might have been quicker to pounce on or defy the hard-line Hindus who had made it compulsory in the district schools to salute the Congress flag, sing songs which had a Hindu rather than an Indian national connotation, and to teach history in a religious rather than political context. It had been this more than anything throughout the country that had alerted the Muslims to the dangers of a Hindu-raj succeeding a British raj and which had provided Jinnah with the kind of political ammunition he'd been so short of'.[13] This spirit of dissension is also seen in one of the letters written by MAK's daughter, who, along with her husband Hydyatullah, had taken the stance of an ardent Leaguist and separatist. How the problem of the division of India was severe is reflected in the letter of MAK's daughter. She writes to her father:

> Tomorrow we are having a party to listen to Wavell on the radio which I expect will be the usual guff, everyone knows he is going to announce the elections. Guzzy says he has no alternative but that the results will surprise him and force him to recognize the reality of the problems that divide the country.[14]

This problem is further highlighted in the talk between MAK and his son Sayed. How the feeling of the separation of the country was deeply rooted in the minds of the people is made clear in Sayed's views. He says to his father:

> It is not a country. It is two countries. Perhaps it is many countries, but primarily it is two. If I'm not wanted in one perhaps I shall be wanted in the other.[15]

The rift between Hindus and Muslims is further noticed in Sayed's observation of the Congress Party. He does not approve of MAK's being a staunch member of the Congress which, he believes, is a communal party. He means to say that his father should quit the Congress Party and join the League. How the Muslims will suffer under the rule of Congress is pointed out by Sayed in the following words:

> They will hand us over to Gandhi and Nehru and Patel - and then where will you be, father? How can you trust Congress as a whole? How can you imagine that just because you've been useful to them in the past you - a Muslim - will be allowed to remain useful when they have power? They will squeeze you out at the first convenient opportunity. Congress is a Hindu party whatever they pretend. They will exploit us as badly as

the British have done, probably worse. There's only one answer and that is to seize what we can for ourselves and run things our own way from there.[16]

This makes it clear how the Muslims were keen on getting Pakistan, a separate state for themselves. How the Hindu-Muslim clash had reached its peak is recurrently brought to our notice. It is once again found in Sayed's talk to his father:

> When you say my military career is finished, I would agree with you. It would be finished if the British stay and finished if we merely substitute a Hindu for a British raj. It would be finished because I'm a Muslim and they hate us. Also they hate each other. A Hindu from UP hates a Hindu from Bengal and both hate a Hindu from the South. A Hindu raj would be a catastrophe. They have nothing to hold them together. They hate and envy us mostly because we have such a thing. We have Islam. It will be madness not to resist them. The only thing that matters in this world, father, is power. We must grasp our own. Surely it is true you have been thinking of this too? Please, do not be too-proud. I do not want to see you become neglected and bitter in your old age.[17]

However, MAK decides to remain a Congressman by not joining Jinnah and therefore he writes to Gandhiji that he had no doubts whatsoever about their commitment to the cause of freedom and unity and non-violence to which he had given not only his life's work but also inspiration to rest of them. He also assures him that he would never abandon the cause.[18] But these views are ridiculed when Scott recurrently points out the rift between Hindus and Muslims which, Scott believes, was a problem very difficult for the Congress to tackle with. That Scott does not believe in the ability of the Congress and Gandhi, probably with the exception of Nehru, is reflected in Perron's talk with Purvis, a member of an economic advisory mission to the Government of India. We learn about this in the following account given by Purvis:

> The place is still feudal, Perron. And so far as I can see the only man of influence who's worried about that is whatever

the chap's name is, Nehru, but he is a Brahmin aristocrat and can hardly speak any language but English,' and against him you have to set the Mahatma and his bloody spinning wheel. Spinning wheel: In 1945. For God's sake, what's the man at? In the past twenty five years he's done as much to keep the country stuck in the mud with his village industry fixation as the whole bloody raj put together.[19]

In pointing out the limitations of Gandhi and consequently the Congress Party Scott shares the views of John Masters, his contemporary who, like him, believes in the values of the Raj. In his famous work, *The Road Past Mandalay*, Masters records how the Congress's campaign never reached the countryside:

In the course of a thousand miles walked through the country between Jhansi and Jubbulpore I questioned several score villagers in different places as to what they knew about the political situation in India, and the war. Most had heard of the war. Two had heard of the Indian National Congress and three of Gandhi.[20]

Thus, Scott makes his point that it would be difficult for the Congress to manage with all the problems after it takes over from the British and, in a way, justifies the superiority of the Raj which, he thinks, had created a particular political order in India.

In this context he discusses various ideas the British implemented in connection with the betterment of the Indians. His intention is to point out that though these ideas were progressive they were not successful due to the lack of agreement on the part of the Indians and ultimately it resulted in the partition of India which was accompanied by the communal holocaust.

He means to say that had the Indians accepted the British ideas there would not have been the tragedy. The failure of the British ideas is expressed through the brilliant use of cartoons in the novel. All these ideas - Simla Conference, Cabinet Mission, June 3 Plan, etc. - are dealt with in a chronological order.

The first is the Simla Conference. At the opening of the novel Scott describes how the Simla Conference ended in a fiasco 'the Conference opened on June 25 and did not break down until July 14, an unexpectedly long time in the opinion of many English officials for Congress and Muslim League views on the composition of a new Indianised Executive Council or interim government to prove irreconcilable. The Viceroy, Lord Wavell, admitting failure, blamed himself and begged that there should be no recriminations. Subsequently, in press conference, the leader of the All India Congress Party, a Muslim, blamed the leader of the Muslim League for the unending nature of his claim for the League's right to nominate all Muslim members of the proposed executive council and blamed the British Government for not having foreseen that the conference would break down if one party were given the right to veto on nominations and therefore the opportunity to hold up the country's progress to autonomy.' [21] If we compare this account with that given by a noted Indian historian, V.D. Mahajan, [22] we find that Scott has not distorted the historical facts. He has maintained accuracy in the names of the persons and the dates on which particular things happen. However, there is a difference of opinion regarding the date of the commencement of the conference. According to Mahajan, the conference began on 26th June, 1945, whereas Scott thinks it began on 25th of June, 1945. However, this difference is negligible. What is important here is Scott's British point of view behind the recreation of this historical event.

Scott's viewpoint is revealed through his treatment of MAK, a Muslim Congressman and an ex-Chief Minister of the pre-war government of the province of Ranpur. He was the first among the members of the conference who left Simla to consider the situation in private. Like several other Congress politicians Mr Kasim was not seen in public for nearly three years. It was supposed that MAK was tempted to join the Muslim League. This feeling is recreated by Scott by making use of a cartoon that appeared in the local newspaper. After the conference ended in disagreement, MAK left the Cecil Hotel guarded from reporters by a small but efficient entourage headed by his younger son, Ahmed. He ignored the questions shouted at him. Safe in his car at last he snubbed the young man from the *Civil and Military Gazette* who got close enough to the window to say, "Minister, is Pakistan now inevitable?" by commanding Ahmed to put up the glass and pull down the blinds.

The lowering down of the blinds caught the imagination of an Indian cartoonist who portrayed 'the car (identified as that of the exChief Minister by the initials MAK on one of its doors) with all its windows, including the driver's, shuttered and making off at high speed (smoke rings from the exhaust) from a once imposing but now crumbling portal inscribed 'Congress' towards a distant horizon with a sun marked 'Hopes of Office' rising behind a broken down bungalow on whose rickety verandah the Leader of the Muslim League, Mr Jinnah could be seen conferring with several of his offices.'[23] The cartoon ridicules MAK because so far he was presented as a staunch Congressman but now he is presented as if his belief is shaken by the hope of getting office by joining the League. It is further illustrated in one more cartoon drawn by the same cartoonist.

After the conference was over MAK went to the Nawab of Mirat instead of his own house on the Kandipat road. This was an indication of his evasive behaviour which inspired the cartoonist to a further interpretation of his behaviour. 'In the new cartoon MAK was shown sitting cross-legged at a low table in the company of the Nawab and Mr Jinnah. The table heavily spread with a feast, was labelled 'Islam'. Beneath it, only head and arms visible, was the struggling body of Free India. From behind the pillar the puckish face of Winston Churchill peered, the head sporting a Jinnah-shaped Fez to depict the English leaders' alleged preference for Muslims and sympathy with their aspirations, the face smoothed by an expression of satisfaction at the thought that the Princes, those loyal Indian supporters of the Crown in two World Wars, and. the Muslim League which had refused to have anything to do with the non-co-operation tactics of the Congress Party, would together - for whatever different reasons - now so bedevil every move the Congress made to force the issue of Indian independence to a conclusion favourable to themselves that British rule could comfortably be extended far enough into the future for the phrase, 'indefinitely if not in perpetuity' not to seem inappropriate'[24] This cartoon further exposes the character of MAK who, in spite of his belief in the Congress, had abandoned the party out of selfishness. It illustrates Scott's point that it was improper to grant freedom to India since she was facing the acute problem of communalism which British only could control.

How the idea of forming the provincial legislatures and central legislature in India did not solve the problem is revealed through the various cartoons drawn by Halki, pseudonym of a young cartoonist Shankar Lal. The Labour Party came to power on 10 July, 1945 after which the King Emperor referred to the Indian affairs in these words:

> In accordance with the promises already made to my Indian
> peoples, my Government will do their utmost to promote

in conjunction with the leaders of Indian opinion, early realisation of full self government in India.[25]

Accordingly Lord Wavell was summoned to London for consultations and he reached there on 25th August, 1945. 'Before his return to India, an announcement was made from London to the effect that fresh elections would be held both for the provincial legislatures and the central legislature in India. Lord Wavell came back to India on 18 September, 1945 and made a broadcast speech on 19 September, 1945 in which he declared that elections would be held in the coming cold weather and after that the Government hoped that ministerial responsibility would be accepted by the political leaders in all the provinces.'[26]

Scott recreates this event by mentioning the cartoons drawn by Halki. The first cartoon is as follows: 'it depicted the then Viceroy, statue-naked on a plinth (inscribed 'Vote') in the attitude of Rodin's Thinker, his bronz shoulders caked with snow. Actually, there were two versions of this unpublished work. The first included in the distant background a hot and sweaty affray between Muslims and Hindus and was captioned 'The Solution?'. The second version, still featuring Wavell as the snow-clad Thinker, omitted the affray but substituted the figure of an undernourished child asleep at the base of the plinth, with one hand grasping his begging bowl. The word 'Vote!' had disappeared from the plinth but reappeared on the side of the empty bowl.'[27] Through this cartoon Scott symbolically suggests that in spite of the introduction of the progressive idea it didn't serve the purpose due to the irreconcilable stance taken by the Congress and the League. Thus, he severely criticises the Indians.

Another cartoon also throws light on the Hindu-Muslim rift and the Indian leaders' apathy of the British idea. 'This cartoon, unpublished and dated 20 September, 1945, was captioned 'Box-Wallah', and portrayed Wavell in the garb of an itinerant Indian merchant and purveyor of ladies' dress material, squatting on his hunkers on the verandah of a European bungalow, recommending his wares to a gathering of memsahibs who bore remarkable resemblances to Bapu, Nehru, Patel, Tara Singh, Maulana Azad and Mohammed Ali Jinnah. Jinnah was sitting somewhat apart from 'her' colleagues, consulting a glossy magazine marked 'The Pakistan Ladies' Home Journal'; but none of them was responding to the pleas of the box-wallah or to the sight of the avalanche of silks and woolens he was flinging hopefully in all directions (lengths marked:

'New Executive Council Indian patterns'; Central Assembly Dress Lengths (for Cold Weather Wear)'; 'Constituent Assembly Fashion Designs, For All Seasons'; 'Provincial Election Lengths: Graded Princes'; 'Dominion Status Fabrics' (Slightly Soiled)'.[28] This cartoon symbolically explains how Jinnah was interested in getting a separate state and how he remained detached from the other leaders of the Congress. It further explains though the British were interested in introducing certain ideas for the benefit of the Indians they were neglected by the Indians, The clothes in the cartoon are silky and woolen which indicate high quality, means, according to Scott, the British ideas were essentially good but since the Indians didn't accept them they were at loss.

This view is further illustrated in the recreation of the Cabinet Mission of 1946. 'On 19 February 1946, Lord Pethic Lawrence made a momentus declaration in the House of Lords in which he announced the decision of the British Government to send a special mission of Cabinet Ministers to resolve the Constitutional deadlock in the country. The members of the Mission were Lord Pethick Lawrence himself. Sir Stafford Cripps, President of the Board of Trade and Mr A.V. Alexander, First Lord of Admirality. The Mission reached Delhi on 24 March, 1946. Prolonged discussions took place between the members of the Mission and the leaders of the Congress and Muslim League. However, the main parties could not come to any mutual understanding. The result was that the members of the Mission had to put forward their own formula for solving the constitutional problem. That formula was embodied in a joint statement issued by the Cabinet Mission and Lord Wavell on 16 May, 1946. After pointing out the impracticability of the Pakistan Scheme the statement of May 16 recommended the new constitution of India should be formed.'[29] Before the members of the Cabinet Mission left India, they issued a statement alongwith Lord Wavell in which they expressed their satisfaction that the work of the making of the constitution would proceed with the consent of the major political parties in India. They regretted that an interim Government-constituting of the various political parties could not be found on account of certain difficulties. It was hoped that after the elections to the Constituent Assembly were over, negotiations would be started for the formation of an interim Government consisting of the representatives of the various political parties.[30]

Scott has highlighted this event by mentioning the following cartoons. 'The first cartoon showed the three sweating members of the mission: Cripps (merely President of the Board of Trade, but difficult to detach from Indian affairs), the Secretary of State (Pethick Lawrence) and the first Lord of the Admirality (Alexander). They were sitting staring at a large map of India which showed the country's provincial boundaries. A legend at one side of the map provided the clue to the different hatchings: perpendicular lines for Hindu majority provinces and horizontal lines for Muslim majority provinces (with a few areas of cross-hatching in the Punjab and Bengal). But nearly one-third of the map remained unhatched. The main caption was: 'A Paramount Question' and this was followed by a sub-caption in the form of a dialogue between the three ministers:

> Sec. of states: I say, Cripps, what do the blanks represent?
> Cripps: God knows.
> Alexander: Perhaps the fellow ran out of ink.'[31]

The meaning of the cartoon is explained by Rowan in the following manner:

> 'Confidentially, it's said to be quite true, that three senior cabinet ministers between them had no idea that the self-ruling princely states, who have individual treaties with the paramount power (the Crown) respecting their rights to their own independence, cover so much of India.'[32]

Here it must be noted that Scott is historically quite authentic so far as the names of the persons and the historical situation is concerned. His intention behind the recreation of the Cabinet Mission is to be seen in the following cartoon, 'dated June 29, 1946, which showed the cabinet mission returning disconsolately to London, climbing aboard a plane labelled 'Imperial Shuttle Service'. The Secretary of State was carrying the Imperial Crown and Cripps was surreptitiously handing him back a large diamond and saying, 'You'd better stick it back in, already'. Halki's inventiveness here lay chiefly in the way he made the three British ministers look like three shady Jews from Amsterdam, and Nehru, Jinnah and Tara Singh look like three equally shady Arab merchants who had come to wave them off but were eyeing each other suspiciously, wondering if the jewel from the crown had been secretly handed over to whichever one of them had offered the highest number of piasters.'[33]

Here the names of the persons are actual historical names. The Imperial Crown is the British Empire and the Jewel from the crown is India herself. Here the problem of succession is dealt with. How the Muslim League and the Congress were very much after taking over from the British is clearly stated in the symbolic cartoon.

The next important event that Scott has recreated is the Direct Action Day which was an action taken by the League to achieve Pakistan but it was marred by the communal riots, especially in Calcutta. Scott makes use of the following cartoons to recreate this event. One of them, for example, was 'sombre pen and ink drawing of Calcutta, captioned 'Direct Action Day', August 16, 1946 and celebrated the result of Jinnah's decision to resort to violence in the belief that the Viceroy had betrayed him by allowing Congress to enter the central interim government without him. In this picture, though, it was difficult to distinguish Muslim dead from Hindu dead Halki had just drawn a pile of bodies, such as might be seen on the streets of Calcutta on any night of the week, except that these were obviously dead, not sleeping; but ordered in rows, like sleepers, in diminishing perspective from a lit to an unlit area. There were several variations on the theme but the most striking was the one that showed the street all but empty. There were no bodies on the pavement, blood-stains adumbrated the shapes of bodies cleared away. In the' background you could just see Bapu, with his staff, accompanied by Jinnah (hands behind back) walking down the road towards the lit area. This carried no caption and was the last of the pictorially sombre cartoons. Sombreness, though, continued in the jokey ones that followed'.[34] Scott has maintained historical accuracy as far as the names and dates are concerned. But the treatment of the event points out that he is interested in pointing out the strong communal disharmony between the Hindus and the Muslims. He also points out the failure of Gandhian principle of non-violence and thus criticises Gandhi. It consolidates Scott's British point of view.

The communal disharmony is further illustrated through few more cartoons. 'A cartoon dated 3 September 1946 marked the occasion of the swearing in of the interim central government headed by Nehru, ostracized by Jinnah and over-shadowed by the' assassination of one of the nominated non-League Muslims, Shafaat Ahmed Khan, which caused riots in Bombay and Ahmedabad. Another in mid-October, celebrated Jinnah's about-face, his decision to co-operate and enter the interim government to protect Muslim interests. To accommodate him three non-League Muslims had to resign.'[35]

Thus, Scott is recurrently pointing out the political impasse between the Hindus and Muslims. This can also be seen in the events after Attlee's statement of February 1947 which was followed by June 3 Plan (1947). In recreating these events Scott has maintained historical accuracy and how it was almost impossible to solve the deadlock between the two races, ultimately the announcement of the separation of India was followed by the communal riots everywhere in India which is realistically described by Scott. For example, he writes:

> There were depressingly familiar reports from Lahore, Amritsar and Calcutta of troubles with the Sikhs and of murders and arson, and equally depressing commentaries on the harrowing experiences of some of the refugees already making their way from what would be Pakistan to what would be India, and vice versa.[36]

The culmination of riots into the death of Ahmed points out Scott's belief how the Indians were uncivilized and unfit to rule their country. It is seen in the following words:

> Perron pushed his way out again. 'Savages', a woman was saying. And a man, 'what do you expect? It's only the beginning. Once we've gone they'll cut each other's bloody throats. Non-violence. Makes you laugh, doesn't it?'[37]

Besides pointing out the severity of the communal riots it also points out Scott's ridiculous treatment given to Gandhian ideals. How the problem of communal disharmony was the most accute problem at the time of Partition can be seen by referring to a few more novelists. For example, Manohar Malgonkar's *A Bend in the Ganges* shows how Gandhi's principle of non-violence was bound to fail perilously as it did with the kind of followers he had. In this respect he writes:

> In the midst of Gandhi's non-violence, violence persists. Violence such as no one has ever seen. That is what awaits this country; the violence bottled up in those who pay lip service to non-violence.[38]

We must note here that unlike Scott, Malgonkar does not reject Gandhi's principles. In *Train to Pakistan* (1956), Khushwant Singh gives a graphic picture of the nation in its most painful and brutal process of partition which came with the fulfilment of the country's long-sought objective of freedom. However, unlike Scott, he does not denounce the process or pleads the British Raj but justifies the violence and says:

> Consciousness of the bad is an essential pre-requisite to the promotion of the good.[39]

Though these writers show a critical attitude by bringing to light the darker aspects that marred the struggle it must be mentioned here that even this critical attitude is imbued in depth with a spirit of nationalism. On the contrary, Scott's critical attitude towards the struggle is created out of his moral justification of the Raj. And therefore, throughout the *Raj Quartet* one gets the feeling that because Scott considers the Raj an important phase in the British imperial history he is seriously preoccupied with the justification of it. He, therefore, says at the time of Partition:

> Finally, with one swift stroke the desired disconnection was achieved. What the English electorate had done was to float India off (in two parts) into seas they themselves were riding with confidence - the stormy seas of the mid-Twentieth century. Under the Raj, India had been anchored in the backwaters of a vanished era. Its members now stood beached, surrounded by the detritus of their cancelled occupation and in possession of nothing but their unchanged belief in the value of the product which they had watched devalued under their very eyes: new and improved beyond recognition - India divided into two and already red with the blood of communal massacre.[40]

Here we notice that Scott is regrets the way in which the Raj ended. The British had never expected a violent end of their rule and as Scott is very seriously committed to the British vision of India he deeply regrets the massacre that accompanied the Partition. Thus, it can be said that Scott's several years' scholarly absorption in the British India is meant for a very significant reason,' i.e., his belief that the British withdrawal, though, inevitable, should not have ended in the tragedy of human life. Human relations are important for him and the transfer of power at the cost of human relations is something that disturbs him. It becomes obvious from the following lines why he did not like the violent actions of the Indians:

> It was the element of scornful rejection implicit in every violent challenge to authority which hurt most deeply and blighted the tendrils of affection which entwined and supported the crumbling pillars of the edifice.[41]

Moreover, his views coincide with those of Leonard Mosley who says:

> That their work should end in the division of the country into two separate nations was not something which any sincere British Official in India could contemplate without abhorence.[42]

The novel is also important so far as it throws light on an operation known as Zipper - an operation related to the invasion and liberation of Malaya. The recreation of the activities of Zipper are important because in the opinion of Richard James, who was engaged in the planning of this operation in Bombay, the Zipper was one of the least known of the war. In this context James has further mentioned his opinion about the Zipper which proves how realistic Scott is in the recreation of history:

> We sat in our offices and tried to find, among other things, the best place to land, getting our information from intrepid men who went ashore and fingered the beaches. The place we chose was of such remarkable unsuitability that the enemy were amazed when they saw it. We were billeted in boarding houses, and it was one of these that I heard the news of Hiroshima. The chance for gallantry was gone, but and no one regretted it.[43]

Paul Scott describes how the expedition 'Operation Zipper' landed on Morib Beach near Port Swettenham. I am grateful to him. I landed in one of the last waves; and believe it or not, his is the first detailed account I have read of how the landing went off....

> The sea journey from Bombay to Port Swettenham was very pleasant. The atom bomb had forced the Japanese to give up. So, in stead of looking ahead with apprehension, I looked back and recollected in the comparative tranquility of a troopship my weary, and ultimately I think rather pointless, wanderings in North Burma under General Wingate. I wrote much of it down in those few days a manuscript that has been rejected by all the best publishers. May be they were right. But I am comforted by the fact that a similar —fate befell a book - a much more substantial writer - Paul Scott's own first novel. Until one wise man finally said 'Yes' and was rewarded with *The Raj Quartet*.[44]

Thus, a glowing tribute paid by James to Scott indicates how minutely Scott was dealing with the historical situations, the fact that enriches his historical imagination.

In this way, taking *The Raj Quartet* into account, we can state that Paul Scott's vital concern with the slow disintegration of the imperial vision in India is a significant probing into the historical aspect of the last years of British India. *The Raj Quartet* is treated as historical set of novels not only in the sense that it moves the reader and quickens and sharpens his sensibilities as put forth by Max Beloff[45] but also in the sense that it interprets the immediate past history with reference to the present time. The comparison is between the British India and the Independent India, twenty five years after the British departure. According to Scott, the position of India now is not better than that of the British India. This view gets clear expression in the following lines:

> That the major promise, independence, had been fulfilled was cold comfort. They wished their lost charge well, but had forebodings. Perhaps many of those who are still alive think they were right, that things are not ordered as well as they used to be. But the world for which the Raj prepared and conditioned India is not the one in which, like the English, she struggles to survive.[46]

NOTES AND REFERENCES

1   Paul Scott, "The Raj," Frank Moraes & Edward Howe (Ed.) *India* (Delhi: Vikas, 197 4), p. 85.

2   *Ibid.*

3   Webster Schott, rev. of *A Division of the Spoils* by Paul Scott, *New York Times Book Review*, October 12, 1975, p. 34.

4   *Ibid.*

5   Avrorn Fleishman, *The English Historical Novel; Walter Scott to Virginia Woolf* (Baltimore & London: Johns Hopkins Press, 1971), p. 4.

6   Paul Scott, *A Division of the Spoils* (Frogmore: Panther, 1975), p. 105.

7   *Ibid.*

8   *Ibid.*

9   Patrick Swinden, *Paul Scott; Images of India* (London: Macmillan,- 1980), pp. 72-73.

10   Paul Scott, *A Division of the Spoils* (Frogmore: Panther 1975), p. 165.

11   *Ibid.*

12   *Ibid.*, p. 4O7.

13   *Ibid.*, p. 393.

14   *Ibid.*, p. 397.

15   *Ibid.*, p. 431.

16   *Ibid.*, p. 432.

17   *Ibid.*

18   *Ibid.*, p. 449.

19   *Ibid.*, p. 32.

20   John Masters, *The Road Past Mandalay* (London; 1961), p. 134.

21   Paul Scott, *A Division of the Spoils* (Frogmore: Panther, 1975), p. 3.

22   Vidya Dhar Mahajan, *Pakistan*, Chapter XXXVI, H.H. Dodwell (Ed.), *The Cambridge History of India*, Vol. VI, *The Indian Empire* (Delhi: S. Chand & Co.), pp. 848-S49.

23   Paul Scott, *A Division of the Spoils* (Frogmore: Panther, 1975), p. 4.

24   *Ibid.*, p. 6.

25   Vidya Dhar Mahajan, Chapter XXXIV; Constitutional Changes from 1919 to 1969, H.H. Dodwell (Ed.), *The Cambridge History of India,* Vol. VI, *The Indian Empire* (Delhi: S. Chand & Co.), p. 677.

26   *Ibid..*

27 Paul Scott, *A Division of the Spoils* (Frogmore: Panther, 1975), p. 456.

28 *Ibid.*, p. 457.

29 Vidya Dhar Mahajan, <u>Chapter XXXIV; Constitutional Changes from 1919 to 1969</u>, H.H. Dodwell (Ed.), *The Cambridge History of India* Vol. VI, *The Indian Empire* (Delhi: 3. Chand & Co.) pp. 678-679.

30 <u>*Ibid*</u>, p. 682-683.

31 Paul Scott, *A Division of the Spoils* (Frogmore: Panther, 1975), pp. 459-460.

32 *Ibid.*, p. 460.

33 *Ibid.*

34 *Ibid.*, pp. 461-462.

35 *Ibid.*, p. 462.

36 *Ibid.*; p. 522.

37 *Ibid.*, p. 586.

38 Manohar Malgonkar, *A, Bend in the Ganges* (London: Hamish Hamilton, 1964), (London: Pan Books, 1967), p. 98.

39 Khushwant Singh, *Train to Pakistan* (Bombay: Pearl Publications, 1957), p. 149.

40 Paul Scott, "The Raj", Frank Moraes & Edward Howe (Ed.) *India* (Delhi: Vikas Publishers, 1974), p. 88.

41 Paul Scott, <u>*The Towers of Silence*</u> (Frogmore: Panther, 1973), p. 82.

42 Leonard Mosley, *The Last Days of the British Raj* (Bombay: Jaico, 1971), p. 8.

43 Richard James, "In the Steps of Paul Scott," *The Listener*, 8 March, 1979, p. 36O.

44 *Ibid.*

45 Max Beloff, "The End of the Raj: Paul Scott's Novels as History," *Encounter*, May 1976, Vol. XLVI, No. 5.

46 Paul Scott, "The Raj", Frank Moraes and Edward Howe (Ed.) *India* (Delhi: Vikas Publishers, 1974), p. 88.

CHAPTER V

Post-*Raj Quartet* Novel

Staying on

STAYING ON

Staying On (1977)

Staying On (1977), which was awarded the Booker Prize, one of England's most prestigious awards, can be regarded as a sequel to Paul Scott's *magnum opus, The Raj Quartet.* Scott himself justifies in the following words why he calls it essentially a post-script:

> Yes, postscript is just about right. Obviously when you spend ten years doing a long sequence more goes into the waste-paper basket than goes on to the page. And perhaps from all this wastage emerge certain people that you've become rather fond of, but you can only use in a separate way - marginal people like the Smalleys. I think I must have thrown away about 50 pages on Lucy Smalley's emotional hang ups which wouldn't fit in, say, to *The Towers of Silence.*[1]

However, it is not just the continuation of the minor characters that make it a sequel. Or, in the words of John Leonard, it cannot be a sequel because 'the Smalleys were so peripheral in the quartet that most readers would not have bothered to notice them at all - the not-very talented British colonel and his dull, if efficient lady'.[2] I regard it a sequel in the sense that Scott continues his ideological stance further in this novel. Like *A Division of the Spoils,* the last of *The Raj Quartet* novels, all the while he is trying to establish the fact that the world for the Raj prepared India is not the one in which she struggles to survive.[3] And this is done with the basic belief in the British superiority, especially the quality of integrity in them.[4] This clearly points out Scott's view as a colonizer.

It is the story of an old British couple, Tusker and Lucy Smalley who played just meagre roles in *The Raj Quartet.* They decide to stay on in India after the Independence thinking that their pension will bring higher standard of living in India. They are staying in the Lodge, an annexe of the Smith's, a hotel in Pankot, a small hill-station once the British regimental depot. Lucy writes about their life-history after Independence to Sarah, who, in London, is settled with Guy Perron, the historian:

> Tusker and I remained at Rose Cottage until early in 1949. You may remember he was invited to stay on for a year or

two on contract with the new Indian Government. When he finally retired he took a commercial job with Smith Brown and Mackintosh in Bombay. The firm sent him home on a short business trip in 1950, and naturally I went with him, but that's the only time I've been in England since first coming out over 40 years ago. It seems so strange to me, put like that. Tusker finally retired about ten years ago when he was sixty and we've been back in Pankot for most of that time and are now literally the last of the permanent British residents on station. Quite a lot of people pass through from time to time, though young people from home and of course tourists, and we have a number of good friends among the Indian officers and their wives.[5]

This description obviously points out Scott's concern with the depiction of the British characters whose experience of post-Independence Indian scene owes its relationship to the British Raj.

The plot of the novel, revolves around the Smalleys' affairs in the hill-station culminating in the Colonel's death. Mrs Bhoolabhoy, a Punjabi lady, the proprietress of the hotel, sends the note of eviction to the Colonel asking him to leave the Lodge and look for an alternative accommodation. The Colonel cannot tolerate the shock of humiliation and dies of a massive coronery. Thus, the plot itself suggests how seriously Scott is occupied with the theme of tragic fate of the Britishers in India.

At the outset one is faced with a crucial question: how can the novel be treated as a historical novel since it deals with the contemporary plight of the British in India? Or, in what way is it related to the past, i.e., the British Raj? The answer to these questions is that it can be treated as a historical novel in the sense that it comments on the moral justification of the Raj which we learn through the technique of comparison between the pre-Independence and post-Independence Indian scenario, the same technique that Scott uses predominantly in *The Jewel in the Crown*. However, *The Jewel in the Crown* takes into account the period of early 'sixties whereas *Staying On* deals with early seventies, i.e., India under Mrs Indira Gandhi's reign before1977, the period of turbulence during the last days of the British Raj being common to both of them.

Thus, so far as the recreation of the past is concerned, the nature of' this recreation is easily divisible on two levels, first, the direct recreation of the past which is mainly done through Lucy's imaginary conversations with David Turner, the prospective visitor to India, her correspondence with Sarah and Tusker's annotating the library book entitled *A Short History of Pankot* by Edgar Maybrick, B.A. LRM, Privately Printed, and secondly, the recreation of the past done through the comparison of the post-Independence Indian scene with that of the pre-Independence and, mainly through the views of the characters who have experienced both the Indias.

As pointed out by Mackinlay Kantor a historical novelist dives deep into the past life and gives a picture of social scene of the time concerned.[6] In the present novel, in this context, Scott has highlighted the rigid levels of hierarchy in British India. How, in those days, the consideration of seniority mattered much and how the human relations were based on hierarchy is shown in one of Lucy's imaginary conversations with Mr Turner. She says:

> And there were those rigid levels of the hierarchy. Put it this way Mr Turner, if you were a captain's. wife there were always other Captain's wives whose husbands were senior. Even a day or two's seniority mattered. You were supposed to know, you were supposed to find out and if you didn't know they made it plain you'd made a gaffe. And above them were the Major's wives. And when Tusker became a major then there were senior Mrs Majors not to mention- Mrs Colonels and Mrs- Brigadiers-and Mrs. Generals all living in that heady atmosphere of the upper air.[7]

Here we must note that Scott is not critical of the British people as a whole but his attack is only on the hidebound nature of the memsahib, the point that remembers us of Mildred Layton who, at times, is criticised by Scott for being unmindful of the Raj-values.

As far as the social scene is concerned Scott makes note of the Eurasian community in India, though, of course, only casually. The character of Susy Williams, a hair-dresser, makes him think of the history of the entire Eurasian community. In his opinion, most of the Eurasians were 'the off-spring of sad and reprehensible liaisons between native women or women of mixed blood and British Other Ranks.'[8] That Scott considers the origin of the Eurasians in a liaison that is 'sad and reprehensible' expresses his detestation of the community. In other words, he strongly believes in the distinct identity of the British.

The role of servants in the British Raj is also a matter of consideration for Scott. How the job of a servant was treated respectable and how the servants were proud of having traditions of them is recorded by Scott in the following lines:

> Personal servants, although no longer de riguer, were nevertheless a status symbol. As such you stood behind your Sahib, or your Memsahib, got nicely pissed in the kitchen, passing to and fro, and anyway had the thrill of doing things in the way your father had done them and his father before him, even though the Sahibs and Memsahibs at the long gleaming table were mostly as black as you were yourself.[9]

But owing to the British withdrawal from India the servants had to suffer in the post-Independence Indian social structure which is made clear in the thoughts of Ibrahim, the Smalleys' servant. Scott states:

> Ibrahim regretted the passing of the days of the raj which he remembered as days when the servants were treated as members of the family, entitled to their good humours and bad humours, their sulks, their outbursts of temper, their right to show who was really boss, and their right to their discreetly appropriated perks, the feathers they had to provide for the nest when the nest they presently inhabited was abandoned by homeward-bound employers. Ibrahim had been brought up in such a nest. He still possessed the chits his father had been given by Colonel Moxon Greize and a photograph of Colonel and Mrs Moxon Greize with garlands round their necks Going Home, 1947.[10]

Here the image of Indians as servants as depicted by Scott illustrates his idea of paternalism in which the British considered their relationship with Indians as the relationship between father-mother and child. Here he is not critical of the Indians because as servants they acted as their children.

One of the most important characteristic features of a historical novel is, as pointed out by Fleishman, that 'the individual lives of the characters are shaped by a specific historical period'.[11] Or, in the words of Prescott, 'they are the creatures of their own time'.[12] In this context it is significant to see how the British Raj made the British in India conscious of their superiority - the 'pukka' element in them which is to be seen in the following lines:

> The Sahib and Memsahib had been pukka-log in the days of
> the raj, had been in India for forty years and although still
> pukka they were often very peculiar, like most old people.[13]

How the British were very much conscious of the pukka element in their character is shown in the musings of Lucy. After having stayed on in India almost for forty years she is afraid of having lost the pukka element in her personality. She, therefore, says to Perron:

> I yearn for you because simply by being here in this house you
> will be the catalyst I need to bring me back into my own white
> skin which day by day, week by week, month by month, year
> after year, I have felt to be increasingly incapable of containing
> me, let alone of acting as defensive armour.[14]

This consciousness of being white suits to the basic consideration of the Britishers as superior people. It is also to be seen when Lucy remembers the old race of British Sahibs and Memsahibs 'smiling if they found anything not quite pukka.'[15] She regrets the departure of the pukka British Sahibs who were substituted by the new Indian ones. Scott, therefore, writes:

> 'Watching them, Lucy realized that nothing had changed
> for her, because there was this new race of Sahibs status and
> connexion wno-had taken the place of Generals and Mrs
> Generals, and she and Tusker had become for them almost as
> far down in the social scale as the Eurasians were in the days
> of the raj.[16]

Further Scott has pointed out the pukka element in the relationship between the Sahib and the servant during the Raj which is not seen in the

Indian Sahib's treatment to his servants. So as to illustrate this point he has taken Ibrahim's case for example. To Ibrahim the difference between being treated by the men like Dr Mitra as if he were merely a machine and an anonymous one at that, and being sworn at by a Sahib like Tusker showed the distinction between a real sahib and the counterfeit. 'The same kind of distinction between a real memsahib and a self-appointed one was apparent when you compared Lucy mem with Mrs Bhoolabhoy'.[17] In this way, even in the small things like the treatment given to the servants Scott has pointed out the superiority of the British.

Complementary to the pukka element is the British conscious ness of integrity in their character. How it was treated important by the British is explained in the following conversation between Ibrahim and Lucy:

> "An Englishman's word is as good as his bond because he is known throughout the world to be an honest man." "Honest because British, Memsahib." "Yes, Ibrahim. But that is all so long ago."[18]

Against this background Scott recreates how the British Raj came to an end and what legacy the British left for the Indians. For example, he throws light on the communal riots and effects of the partition of India. As far as the recreation of the communal riots is concerned he points out how the ruthless killings of Muslims by Hindus and *vice versa* took place. For example, in one of her imaginary conversations with Turner Lucy remembers the attack on Ahmed and feels very sorry for him. Her expression is noted in the following words:

> And she said oh, that's Mr Perron (she must have said), who was with us in the carriage when the Hindus stopped the train and dragged Muslims out, he's come upto see how we all are before flying home, come and meet him. [19]

Further Scott has recorded how the refugees had to face the crisis which is exemplified in the case of the owners of the Shiraz, a hotel in Pankot. Besides the Shiraz, they owned a new hotel in Ranpur, one in Mayapore, and another down in Mirat. They also owned a small chain of restaurants called the Go-Go Inns which were specialized in Punjabi food. The effect of Partition on these people is referred to in the following lines:

All the businessmen concerned in these enterprises had come from the Western Punjab in 1947 when it became part of Pakistan at the time of Independence and Partition, and had arrived in India penniless, they said. Mrs Bhoolabhoy's first husband was believed to have come from there, having "lost his all" in the riots between Muslims and Hindus.[20]

Scott also describes how the Independence was celebrated in India in 1947. He describes, for instance, such a ceremony in Pankot. 'The Independence was celebrated on the evening of August Fourteen, Nineteen Forty Seven on the parade ground of the Pankot Rifles. The whole place was floodlit. There was still one small British Contingent on Station, a mixed bunch. They marched on last after all the Indian troops had marched on. There was a band. That was a pretty scratch affair too, but they seemed inspired by the occasion. They played all the traditional material British Music. Then there were some Indian pipers, and a Scottish pipe-major. They played 'The Flowers of Forest'. One by one all the floodlights were put out leaving just the Flagpole lit with the Union Jack flying from it. Colonel Layton and the new Indian colonel stood at attention side by side. Then the Jack was hauled down inch by inch in utter, utter silence. There was no sound otherwise until on the stroke of midnight the Indian flag began to go up and then the band began to play the new Indian National anthem and all the crowds out there in the dark began to sing the words and when the flag was up there flying and the anthem was finished you never heard such cheering clapping.'[21] It is seen here that Scott is quite objective in the recreation of the celebration of the event of Independence. It is also significant to note that since the event and dates are quite identifiable and accurate they make his novel essentially historical one if considered from Nield's point of view who believes that a novel is rendered historical by the introduction of dates, personages or events to which identification can be really given.[22]

However, it is equally important to note Scott's point of view behind the recreation of these events. Scott's moral justification of the British Raj defines his point of view. All the while he speaks about the British legacy to India which means he thinks from the British point of view only. It is interesting to learn how Scott feels about the relationship between Nehru and Dickie Mountbatten. He says that 'in 1947 when the British handed over and the Indians started killing each other and would have fallen apart if Mountbatten hadn't been backed up by men like Nehru who was an aristocrat, an old Harrovian and a thorough gentleman and by an army whose senior officers were mostly Sandhurst men awfully reliable.'[23] Scott's appreciation of Nehru because he was educated at Harrow and the senior officers because they were trained at Sandhurst clearly indicates Scott's love for English things. This point is further illustrated when he thinks of the British legacy to the Indians. In this context, he obviously maintains:

> There really wasn't a single aspect of the nice civilized things in India that didn't reflect something of British influence. Colonel Menektara had impeccable English manners, as did his wife who was in many ways as big a bitch as Mildred Layton had been, but this comforted Lucy since it indicated continuity of civilized behaviour, and as a wife of a retired Colonel herself she was in a position to give delicately as good as she delicately got which meant that she and CooCoo Menektara understood one another perfectly.[24]

The point of British legacy to India is further illustrated by the author when he points out how the services of the senior British officers were required at the time of transition. It was one of the reasons why Tusker and Lucy Smalley stayed on in India after Independence. He, therefore, holds how important the British training was to the Indians. He says:

> You'll find it's in the army where the clearest evidence of our influence for good is found, but then of course many of the senior Indians in 1947 were Sandhurst trained. Some of them became generals overnight.[25]

Thus, the entire part of the British legacy to the Indians points out Scott's love for English things and the superiority of the British people to the Indians.

As has been already pointed out, the novel oscillates between the British India and the present-day India - a remarkable technique that we find in *The Jewel in the Crown* which enables the author compare the past with the present and show his priorities. It is a remarkable technique of the historical novel writing because, as pointed out by Pearce, 'there is an inevitable relationship between the past and the present since the literary work carries the past into the present'[26] Or, in the words of Fleishman:

> The men of the present look back to the men of the past not merely to understand them but to understand themselves; historical thought is seen here as moving from the present to the past in order to be reflected back to the present with enhanced power of meeting the problems of life.[27]

Within this point of reference we will examine how Scott has recreated the British Indian history in the context of the present day India. At the outset, one thing that strikes us is that the past is remembered by the British because of their uneasy present. They are not regarded as important figures in India after Independence. Moreover, they have to suffer a lot of humiliation at the hands of Indians. Here the novelist is interested in the tragic end of the Britishers, their feelings and emotions – the things, according to Prescott, which are absent from the formal history and hence the special magic of fiction.[28]

The tragedy of the British can be seen in Lucy's thoughts. For example, she says, "We are people in shadow... And the dew does not so much nourish us as aggravate our rheumatism and our tempers."[29] Her unhappiness in life can also be seen when she says, "I have had rather a sad life... Yes, from the beginning I had a sad life."[30] How the British were insulted by the Indians after Independence is noted by Scott. For instance, once Mrs Bhoolabhoy interrupts Lucy during lunch and rudely asks her for the return of the garden implements which, she believes, were taken without her permission.[31] How the British were treated with vindictive attitude is also to be seen when, for example, Mr Bhoolabhoy tells Mrs Bhoolabhoy that the Smalleys cannot afford to stay in the Shiraz, a new hotel in Pankot, she suddenly bursts out:

> What they can afford or not afford does not interest me. It is no concern of mine. When they ruled the roost our concerns did not enter their heads. It is tit for tat.[32]

At the base of all this recreation of the past there lies the grim reality of the loss of empire by the British. How India affected the British badly is to be seen in Lucy's introspection:

I feel that India brought out all my very worst qualities. I don't mean this India, though heaven help me. I sometimes don't see a great deal of difference between theirs and the one in which I was a memsahib, but our India, which kept me in my place bottled up and bottled in, and brainwashed me into believing that nothing was more important to do everything my place required me to do to be a perfectly complementary image of Tusker and his position. Do *no* less, certainly no more, except to the extent that one might judge doing an allowable bit more might help him.[33]

It is seen here how Scott believes that in spite of the fact that to serve in India was not congenial to the British they served India for the betterment of the Indians and even then they are neglected by the Indians after Independence. At the root of the sadness of the Britishers lies their strong feeling of alienation which is presented in Lucy's thoughts about her life after Tusker's death. After his death Lucy feels utter loneliness amidst the alien land of Indians. In this situation she feels that Turner's presence would be a godsend to her. Her last speech symbolically speaks of the tragic end of the British people in India:

- but now, until the end, I shall be alone, whatever I am doing, here as I feared, amid the alien corn, waking, sleeping, alone for ever and ever and I cannot bear it but mustn't cry and must must get over it but don't for the moment see how, so with my eyes shut, Tusker, I hold out by hand, and beg you, Tusker, beg, beg you to take it and take me with you. How can you not, Tusker? Oh, Tusker, Tusker, Tusker, how can you make me stay here by myself while you yourself go home?[34]

Lucy cannot bear to stay in India without Tusker because it is not the land for which the British Raj had paved path for. This utter sense of frustration makes her leave India once and for all.

It is not only the plight of the British after Independence that Scott is concerned with but it is also the nature of Indians that forms the centre of his recreation. By becoming critical of the Indians he points out the moral superiority of the British. For example, his criticism of Indians can be found in his description of the Indians as follows:

... they (Eurasians) formed an effective and in-depth defence against the strange native tendency to bribery and corruption which, coupled with that other native tendency to indolence, could have made the Indian empire even more difficult to run than it already was.[35]

Or, he becomes critical of the emerging Indian middle class of 'wheelers and dealers,' who, he believes, 'with their chicanery, their corrupt practices, their black money, their utter indifference to the state of the nation, their use of political power for personal gain were ruining the country if not ruining it making it safe chiefly for themselves'.[36] Again he is critical of people like Mrs Desai who always neglect the British and are unreliable. So, Lucy writes to Sarah about Mrs Desai:

> ...it's not much to ask and you can't rely on people like Mrs Desai who's always going to and fro between Delhi, Zurich, London, Paris and New York and comes back loaded with stuff from the duty-free shops and other stuff that if she doesn't smuggle in must cost her a fortune, at the customs not that she can't afford it but she always seems to forget my little requests.[37]

Here even if we don't find any Kiplingesque conflict between East and West as pointed out by Philip Altbach,[38] we do notice that the image of Indians as depicted by Scott is not much different from that of Kipling's who considers Indians as inferior people. However, in this respect we must note that he is never critical of Mrs Indira Gandhi. That Scott regards her as an efficient administrator is obvious when he says:

> Government was very hot on catching people dealing in black money. The Prime Minister herself took a personal interest in putting a stop to it. Tusker was always saying that the Prime Minister was the one person in India capable of ending corruption.[39]

He also believes that 'with such a Prime Minister as Nehru's daughter at the helm one need never fear a dictatorship of generals, such as they'd been forced to have in Pakistan'.[40] But in trying to show Mrs Gandhi's efficiency Scott has shown its roots in the personality of Nehru who was 'an aristocrat, an old Harrovian' - the thing that is English.[41] It does mean that Scott believes that whatever good is found in India owes its origin to the British ideas and institutions. This attitude of Scott defines his point of view, i.e., his strong belief in the superiority of the English people. In this way, it can be stated that though the novel deals with the post-Independence scene it recreates the history of British India which is inevitably linked with the present. Paul Gray, therefore, says that 'what Tusker and Lucy are living through is a tiny version of the experience so central to *The Raj Quartet*.[42]

At this juncture one can compare Scott with Ruth Prawer Jhabvala who, like Scott, was the recepient of the Booker Prize for her *Heat and Dust* in which there are two pictures of India, one of pre-Independence days and another of today. The India of the twenties and thirties of the novel is depicted only as exotic India through foreign eyes with all the strange and bewildering phenomena connected with riots and sati, Nawabs and Maharajas, and eunuchs and holy men. The modern India, as we see it here, is a world of fake sadhus and profane experiences. Though, like *Staying On*, this novel presents India as a detestable place it does not catch the feeling of real India as *Staying On* does. However, in both the novels the image of India appears to be destorted by Western attitudes.

NOTES AND REFERENCES

1   Michael Barber, "Plain Tales from the Raj and other Worlds," *The Times*, Thursday, November 24, 1977.

2   John Leonard, "Love and Death in India," rev. of *Staying On* by Paul Scott, *The New York Times*, July 26, 1977, 'Books of the Times' column.

3   Paul Scott, "The Raj," Frank Moraes and Edward Howe (ed.), *India* (Bombay: Vikas Publishing, 197 4), p. 88.

4   *Ibid.*

5   Paul Scott, *Staying On* (Bombay: Allied Publishers, 1977), p. 64.

6   MacKinlay Kantor, "The Historical Novel," Ireving Stone et al., *Three Views of the Novel* (Washington: Library Congress, 1957), p. 30.

7   Paul Scott, *Staying On* (Bombay: Allied Publishers, 1977), pp. 142-43.

8   *Ibid.*, p. 173.

9   *Ibid.*, p. 33.

10 *Ibid.*, p. 22.

11 Avrom Fleishman, *The English Historical Novel* (Baltimore: Johns Hopkins Press, 2nd ed., 1972), p. lo.

12 Orville Prescott, *In My Opinion: An Inquiry into the Contemporary Novel* (New York: Charter Books, 1963), p. 134.

13 Paul Scott, *Staying On* (Bombay: Allied Publishers, 1977), p. 50.

14 *Ibid.*, p. 92.

15 *Ibid.*, p. 181.

16 *Ibid.*

17 *Ibid.*, p. 22.

18 *Ibid.*, p. 44.

19 *Ibid.*, p. 91.

20 *Ibid.*, p. 12.

21 *Ibid.*, p. 143.

22 Jonathan Nield, *A Guide to Best Historical Novels and Tales* (New York: Burt Franklin, Reprint, 1968), p. XVIII.

23 Paul Scott, *Staying On* (Bombay: Allied Publishers, 1977), p. 79.

24 *Ibid.*

25 *Ibid.*, p. 131.

26 R.H. Pearce, *Historicism Once More; Problems and Occasions* for the American Scholar (Princeton: Princeton Univ. Press, 1964), p. 5.

27   Avrom Fleishman, *The English Historical Novel* (Baltimore: Johns Hopkins Press, 2nd ed., 1972), pp. 13-14.

28   Orville Prescott, *In My Opinion: An Inquiry into the Contemporary Novel* (New York: Charter Books, 1963), p. 134.

29   Paul Scott, *Staying On* (Bombay: Allied Publishers, 1977), p. 31.

30   *Ibid.*, p. 67.

31   *Ibid.*, p. 188.

32   *Ibid.*, p. 163.

33   *Ibid,* p. 142.

34   *Ibid.*, p. 216.

35   *Ibid.*, p. 172.

36   *Ibid.*, p. 80.

37   *Ibid.*, p. 81.

38   Philip Altbach, rev. of *Staying On* by Paul Scott, *Indian Book Chronicle,* November 1, 1978, p. 365.

39   Paul Scott, *Staying On* (Bombay: Allied Publishers, 1977), p. 113.

40   *Ibid.*, p. 79.

41   *Ibid.*

42   Paul Gray, rev. of *Staying On* by Paul Scott, *Time* (110:89), July 18, 1977.

CHAPTER VI

Conclusion

Paul Scott considers progress in history a significant aspect of his art because 'discounting the actual progress in history' there is not much 'to add to *Passage* that a modern writer could consider lastingly important to add'.[1] However, Scott's belief in the progress in history is distinct. It makes him conscious of the superiority of the British. Scott's belief in the racial superiority of the British reflects Herder's views. Herder believes that as a natural being, man is divided into various races of mankind, each closely related to its geographical environment and having its original physical and mental characteristics moulded by that environment. Each race, once formed, is a specific type of humanity which has permanent characteristics depending on its own inbred peculiarities. This racially differentiated humanity is a matrix in which there arises a race whose life in stead of remaining static develops in time into higher and higher forms. In this context Herder contends that in Europe alone human life is genuinely historical, whereas in China or India there is no historical progress but only a static unchanging civilization. Europe is thus considered as a privileged region of human life. Scott's belief in the racial superiority of the British can be summed up in his view that the Indians are incapable of correct (i.e., English style) government.[2]

While in the recreation of the historical events Scott maintains historical accuracy regarding the names of the persons and the events concerned, he depicts them from the British point of view. That is to say, he never criticises the British officials like Cripps or Mountbatten, on the contrary, he is highly critical of All India Congress, Indian National Army, Mahatma Gandhi, Subhas Bose and other Indian leaders. It clearly points out Scott's British point of view. Broadly speaking, Scott's historical imagination seems to have been limited to the state of the British only. Thus, in the view of Fanon, the history which Scott writes 'is not the history of the country which he plunders but the history of his own nation in regard to all that she skims off, all that she violates and starves.'[3] And therefore, even though Antony Copley believes that Salman Rushdie's quest to categorize all recent writing on the British in India as a 'Raj revisionism' is a 'misguided reductionism',[4] there is some truth in it when Rushdie claims that *The Raj Quartet* is an example of 'a continuing delusion of grandeur, Empire revivalism, and more especially, Raj revisionism'.[5]

Even though, on the ideological level, Scott seems to be biased, we cannot neglect his distinction as an artist because the historical novelist is first and foremost an artist and not a historian. Scott is a conventional story-teller who uses all the devices that the imagination usually provides a fictional writer with; drama, suspense, coincidence, romance, etc. The structure of his novels has the conventional stages of exposition, development, climax and denoument, though, at times, his novels become prolix and repetitious. Sometimes the use of flashbacks becomes Scott's favourite device. For example, *Staying On* begins with the death of Tusker Smalley followed by his tragic life in India after Independence. Or, *The Day of the Scorpion* begins with the decadent Muslim life in Independent India followed by the recreation of the British Raj. Scott also creates a good deal of romance in his novels. For instance, the love scenes between Hari and Daphne, Susan and Teddie, the descriptions of Operation Zipper and the royal Shikar illustrate the romantic elements present in Scott's novels.

As far as the characters are concerned Scott tries to do away with the traditional stereotyped images of the 'Sahibs' and the 'Memsahibs'. And in this respect he has succeeded to a large extent. He depicts the Britishers in the turmoil of the last days of the Raj and creates, unlike his predecessors, the tragic figures of the Britishers, In this sense he has created some memorable characters like Daphne Manners, Edwina Crane, Ronald Merrick, Sarah and Susan Layton, Mabel and Mildred Layton, Barbara Batchelor, Lucy and Tusker Smalley, and others. Hence it can be stated that Scott achieves what is lacking in the novels before him, that is, the depiction of the characters in the context of historical situation. Scott's achievement, then, is to break with this ahistorical novelistic tradition of Anglo-Indian fiction. However, most of his British characters seem to be Scott's mouthpieces because all the while Scott has imbued them with the Raj values, for example, paternalism, incorruptibility, the British sense of justice, etc. In doing so he illustrates his point that 'there is a bit of the author in all my characters'.[6] Scott's characterisation is closely related to his historical vision, that is, the moral justification of the Raj. He portrays the Britishers as the persons possessing superior qualities and hence morally fit to rule India. On the contrary, he denounces the Indians and neglects the feeling of nationalism in them, their love for their native values, etc. It is illustrated through the characters of Pandit Baba, Lady Chatterjee, Vidyasagar, Mrs Bhoolabhoy, and others. This stance substantiates Scott's biased viewpoint. However, it cannot be denied that it is mainly through his characters that Scott has created a picture of human activity and that is why he cannot be treated as a merely documentary novelist.

Besides characters, Scott's novels become lively because of his excellent use of places and objects. For example, the Bibighar Gardens is a place which is full of mystery and romance, or, the Rose Cottage is a place which symbolically stands for the tradition of the 'pukka sahibs' in India. The objects like a lace christening shawl or a book of Urdu poems by Gaffur, which are symbolically related to the activities of human beings, definitely add to the artistic devices used by Scott.

The use of internal monologues is one of Scott's favourite artistic devices. These monologues provide revealing insight into the working of the person's mind. And in this respect, the psychological aspect of Scott's characters becomes one of the important features of his art. For example, in *Staying On*, we find monologues in Lucy's frequent imaginary conversations with Mr. Turner, a prospective English visitor to India. It is through these monologues only that we learn about Lucy's state of helplessness and her strong feeling of alienation. In depicting certain scenes Scott shows the skill of a painter. For example, the entire scene of the attack on Miss Edwina Crane and the killing of Mr D.R. Chaudhuri vividly bring before our mind's eye the turbulent nature of the situation during the Quit India movement. Similarly, Susan's act of attempting to kill her baby and Barbie's state of insanity are the scenes that create a lasting impression on the minds of the readers. In the hands of Scott places and landscapes become alive and parade in the novel almost like living characters. For instance, the detailed descriptions of the town of Mayapore, the Bibighar Gardens, the Club and the Gymkhana, give the novel a dimension of painting.

Titles of Scott's novels are invariably symbolic and almost always convey more than the surface meaning. In *The Jewel in the Crown*, for example, 'the jewel' symbolises India and 'the Crown' symbolises the British Empire. In *The Day of the Scorpion*, and *The Towers of Silence*, the symbols of the scorpion and the towers of silence stand for the British Raj, more specifically, the tragic end of it. Similarly, in *The Birds of Paradise*, the caged birds stand for the British in India rendered helpless during the turbulent situation at the end of the Raj. Besides the titles, all his works are pregnant with the symbols of varied types. Thus, considered from the artistic point of view, Scott's distinction as a historical novelist is of high order.

NOTES AND REFERENCES

1   Paul Scott, "India: A Post-Forsterian View", Mary Stocks, (Ed.) *Essays By Divers Hands* (London: OUP, 1970), p. 114.

2   …….. "The Raj", Frank Moraes and Edward Howe (Ed.), *India* (Delhi: Vikas Publishers, 197 4), p. 85.

3   Frantz Fanon, *The Wretched of the Earth* (Harmondsworth: Penguin, 1963), p. 40.

4   Antony Copley, "The Politics of Illusion: Paul Scott's *The Raj Quartet*", *Indo-British Review*, Vol. XI, No. 1, December 1984, p. 58.

5   Quoted from the Editorial of *The Times of India*, "Rushdie's Complaint", April 13, 1984.

6   Caroline Moorehead, "Novelist Paul Scott: Getting Engrossed in the Death-Throes of the Raj" *Times;* October 20, 1975, A Times Profile Column.

SELECT BIBLIOGRAPHY

[This list includes all works mentioned in this study and some others that I found useful but had no opportunity to cite directly. Bibliographical particulars, wherever they occur, indicate particulars of the editions referred to in this study.]

Works by Scott:

Creative:

The Alien Sky. London: Hienemann, 1953.

The Birds of Paradise, London: Hienemann, 1962.

The Jewel in the Crown. Frogmore: Panther Books Ltd., 1966.

The Day of the Scorpion. Frogmore: Panther Books Ltd., 1968.

The Towers of Silence. Frogmore: Panther Books Ltd., 1971.

A Division of the Spoils. Frogmore: Panther Books Ltd., 1975.

Staying On. Bombay: Allied Publishers Pvt. Ltd., 1977.

Critical:

"India: A Post-Forsterian View". Essays By Divers Hands: Being the Transaction of the Royal Society of Literature. Ed. Mary Stocks. London: OUP, 1970, pp. 113-132.

"The Raj". India. Ed. Frank Moraes and Edward Howe. Delhi: Vikas Publishing House Pvt. Ltd., 1974, pp. 70-88.

Works on Scott:

All, Tariq. "Fiction as History, History as Fiction". Indp-British Review, Vol. XI, No. 2, June 1985, pp. 72-78.

Banerjee, Jaqueline. "A Living Legacy: An Indian View of Paul Scott's India". London Magazine, Vol. 20, Nos. 1,2, April, May 1980, pp. 97-104.

Barber, Michael. "Plain Tales from the Raj and Other Worlds". The Times, November 24, 1977.

Beloff, Max. "The End of the Raj: Paul Scott's Novels as History". Encounter, Vol. XLVI, No. 5, May 1976, pp. 65-70.

Chacko, Arun. "Englishman's Love for India (Peter Scott and Paul Scott)". Indian Express, February 9, 1972, p. 3.

Copley, Antony. "The Politics of Illusion: Paul Scott's 'The Raj Quartet'". Indp-British Review, Vol. XI, No. 1, December 1984, pp. 58-73.

Coppola, Carlo. "Attitude Towards Gandhi and Gandhian Ideology in Some Indo-Anglian and Western Novels". South Asian Review, Vol. V, No. 2, July 1981, pp. 88-105.

Couto, Maria. "Midnight's Children and Parents: The Search for Indo-British Identity". Encounter, Vol. LXVIII, No. 2, February 1982.

------ "Clinging to the Wreckage: Raj Fictions". Encounter, Vol. LXIII, No. 3, September, October 1984, pp. 34-40.

Cox, C.B. "The British in India". The Hudson Review, Vol. XXXVII, No. 3, Autumn 1984, pp. 358-362.

Gooneratne, Yasmine. "Paul Scott's 'Staying On': Finale in a Minor Key". The Journal of Indian Writing in English, Vol. 9, No. 2, July 1981, pp. 1-12.

James, Richard Rhodes. "In the Steps of Paul Scott". The Listener, March 8, 1979, pp. 359-60.

Kohli, Indira. "He wrote India Out of His System". The Times of India, July 14, 1985, p. 8.

Leonard, Joha. "Private Lives". An Obituary on Paul Scott. The New York Times, March 8, 1978.

Mahood, M.M. "Paul Scott's Guardians". Indo-British Review, Vol. XI, No. 1, December 1984, pp. 74-86.

Malgonkar, Manohar. "Salute to Paul Scott". An Obituary on Paul Scott. Debonair, May 5, 1978, pp. 50-51.

Mellors, John. "Raj Mahal: Paul Scott's India Quartet". London Magazine, Vol. 15, No. 2, June,July 1975, pp. 62-67,

Moorehead, Caroline. "Novelist Paul Scott: Getting Engrossed in the Death-Throes of the Raj". Times, October 20, 1975, A Times Profile Column.

Narayanan, Gomathi. "Paul Scott's Indian Quartet: 'The Story of a Rape'". The Literary Criterion, Vol. Xiil, No. 4, 1978, pp. 44-53.

Parry, Benita. "Paul Scott's Raj". South Asian Review, Vol. 8, No. 4, July, October 1975, pp. 359-69.

"Rushdie's Complaint". Editorial. The Times of India, April 13, 1984, p.8.

Sethi, Sunil. "'The Raj Quartet': Recasting a Jewel". India Today, May 31, 1982, pp. 132-33.

-Suraiya, Jug. "Relics of the Raj" » Debonair,. April- -k98Q,, ■-.:■. pp. 3'5-38.

Swinden, Patrick. Paul Scott; Images of India. London: Macmillan, 1980.

(The author, who considers Paul Scott to be one of the best English novelists to have emerged since the War, in this brief introduction to Scott's works, tries to highlight Scott's understanding of political as well as psychological issues.)

The Making of 'The Jewel in the Crown'; The Granada Television Series based on Paul Scott's 'Raj Quartet'. London: Granada Publishing Ltd., 1983.

(The book gives an account of the making of the Granada Television Series based on the Raj Quartet. Bamber Gascoigne tells how the cast and the production team prepared for their trip to India and how they fared in Mysore and Simla. James Cameron describes the vivid political^ background to the end of the British Raj. Ken Taylor gives a resume of the story of each of the fourteen episodes. Ronald Gant and M.M. Kgy throw light on Scott as a man and an artist.)

Weinbaum, Francine. "Paul Scott's India: 'The Raj Quartet'". Critique, Vol. 2o, No. 1, 1979, pp. 100-110.

Zorn, Jean G. "Talk With Paul Scott". New York Times, August 21, 1970.

Works on Anglo-Indian Literature

Greenberger, Allen J. The British Image of India: A Study in the Literature of Imperialism, 1880-1960. London: OUP, 1969.

Hemenway, Stephen. The Novel of India; The Ang.1 o. Tndian Novel. Vol. I. Calcutta: Writers Workshop, 1975.

Islam, Shamsul. <u>Chronicles of the Raj: A Study of Literary Reaction to the Imperial Idea Towards the End of t</u>he Rai. London: Macmillan, 1979.

(The book explores the literary reaction to the imperial idea during its decline with reference to the Raj, 1914-1947. Throughout the study Kipling is used as a constant point of reference. The book also includes a study of the works of E M. Forster, B.J. Thompson, George Orwell and John Masters.)

Naik, M.K. <u>et al</u>. The Image of India in Western Creative Writing Dharwar: Karnatak University, 1970.

(This book is an attempt to bring into focus various aspects of Western response to India. The authors discussed here include Kipling, Forster, Eliot, Yeats, Myres, Steinbeck, and others.)

Nicholson, Kai. A Presentation of Social Problems in the <u>Indo-Anglian</u> and Anglo-Indian Novel. Bombay: Jaico, 1972.

Oaten, Edward Farley, <u>a Sketch of Anglo-Indian Literature.</u> London: Kegan Paul, 1908.

Parry, Benita. <u>Delusions and Discoveries; Studies on India in the British Imagination, 188O-.193O</u> . New Delhi: Orient Longman, 1972.

(This book gives a portrait of the British in India with special reference to the study of the works by Flora Annie Steel, Edmund Candler, Kipling, Forster, and othe rs .)

Sencourt, Robert. <u>India in English Literature</u>. London: Simpkin, Marshall, Hamilton, Kent & Co. Ltd., 1925.

Singh, Bhupal. <u>A Survey of Anglo-Indian Fiction</u>. London: Curzon Press, 1934.

Viswanatham, K. <u>India in English Fiction</u>. Waltair: Andhra University Press, 1971.

Bibliographies, Theses and Encyclopaedic Works:

Baker, Ernest A. <u>Guide to Historical Fiction</u>. London: George Routledge & Sons Ltd., 1914.

Bryfonski, Dedria. Ed. <u>Contemporary Literary Criticism</u>. Vol. 9. Detroit-Michigan: Gale Research Co., Book Tower, 1978.

(The volumes give excerpts from criticism of the works of today's novelists, poets, playwrights, and other creative writers.)

Edwards, Paul. Ed. <u>The Encyclopaedia of Philosophy</u>. Vol. III. London: Macmillan, 1967.

(The volume gives the philosophical aspects of historical explanation, a definition of historicism, and discusses the problem of selection of historical facts.)

<u>Encyclopaedia Americana</u>. Vol. 2o. New York: 1963.

(Analyses the distinction between the historical romance and the historical novel with reference to American historical fiction.)

<u>Encyclopaedia Britanica</u>. Vol. 16. London: rept. 1964.

(Gives a comprehensive analysis of the types of historical fiction: romance, fictionalised biography and historical novel proper.)

Gupta Brijen K. <u>India in English Fiction (18OO-1970): An Annotated Bibliography</u>. Methuen: The Scarecrow press, Inc., 1973,

John, A. and Karkala, Leena. <u>Bibliography of Indo-English Literature</u>. Delhi: Nirmala Sadanand Prakashan, 1974.

Joneja, Om Prakash. Coloni<u>al Consciousness in Recent Black American, Indian and African Fiction with Specia</u>l <u>Reference to the Novels of Richard Right, Ralf Ellison</u>, James Baldwin, Raja Rao, R.K. Narayan, Mulk Raj Anand, Chinua Achebe, T.M. Aluko and James Ngugi. Ph.D. Thesis submitted to the Maharaja Sayajirao University of Baroda, 1980.

Khan, A.S. <u>Paul Scott as A Novelist</u>. Ph.D. Thesis submitted to the University of Gujrat.

Locher, Frances Carol. Ed. <u>Contemporary Authors</u>. Vols. 77-80. Detroit-Michigan: Gale Research Co,, Book Tower, 1979.

(The volumes are a bio-bibliographical guide to current writers in fiction, general non-fiction, poetry, journalism, drama, and other fields.)

Logasa, Honnah. <u>Guide to Junior Historical Fiction</u>. 7th Ed. Philadelphia: MeKinley Publishing Co., 1960.

(The book gives an annotated bibliography of the historical fiction with an introduction to the genre.)

Redmond, James, et al. The Year's Work in English Studies. Vol. 59. London: John Murrey, 1980.

Sasikala, C.R. The Indian Novels of Paul Scott: Themes and Treatment. M. Litt. Dissertation submitted to the University of Madras.

Satin, Nora. India in Modern English Fiction with Special Reference to Rudyard Kipling, E.M. Forster and Aldous Huxley. Published Ph.D. Thesis, Norwood Editions, 1976.

(In this dissertation the author studies the image of India that emerges from the fiction of Kipling, Forster and Huxley.)

Sills, David L. Ed. International Encyclopaedia of the Social Sciences. Vol. 3. New York: The Macmillan Co. & the Free Press, 1968.

(The volume gives an important discussion regarding the analysis of historiography and fidelity of records.)

Spenser, Dorothy. Indian Fiction in English. Philadelphia: University of Pennsylvania Press, 1960,

Wilson, James, Ed. Contemporary Novelists. London.;. St. James Press, 1976.

(The volume introduces the works by most of the contemporary novelists. It includes a note on the novels of Paul Scott by Keith Walker.)

Wakeman, John. World Authors: A Companion Volume to Twentieth Century Authors. New York: H.W. Wilson Co., 1975.

Weinbaum, Francine S. Aspiration and Betrayal in Paul Scott's 'The Raj Quartet'. Ph.D. Thesis submitted to the university of Illionois at Urbana-Champaign, 1976.

Yapp, M.E. "The Raj and India". The Illustrated Weekly of India, February 28, 1982. pp. 26-29.

(Yapp discusses the books on India by British authors right from the rash of memoirs published so far, to the official documents on the transfer of power.)

Works on the nature of the historical novel:

Aaron, Daniel. "Fictionalizing the Past". <u>Partisan Review</u>, Vol. XLVII, No. 2, 1980, pp. 231-41.

Allen, Walter. <u>The English Novel</u>. Harmondsworth: Penguin, 1954.

Allott, Miriam. <u>Novelists on the Novel</u>. London: Routledge and Kegan Paul, 1959.

Alter, Robert. "History and Imagination in the Nineteenth Century Novel". <u>Georgia Review</u>, Vol. XXIX, No. 1, Spring 1975, pp. 42-60.

Baker, E.a. <u>The History of the English Novel</u>. Vol. VII. New York: Barnes and Noble Inc., 1957.

Bald, Suresh R. <u>Novelists and Political Consciousness; Literary Expression of Indian Nationalism, 1919-1947</u>. Delhi: Chanakya Publications, 1982.

Baumgarten, Murray. "The Historical Novel: Some Postulates". <u>An Interdisciplinary Journal of Literature, History and Philosophy of History</u>, Vol. 4, No. 2, 1975, pp. 173-82.

Berger, M. Real and Imagined Worlds: The Novel and Social Science, Cambridge: Harward University Press, 1977.

Bergonzi, Bernard. "Fictions of History". <u>The Contemporary English Novel</u>. Ed. Malcolm Bradbury and David Palmer. London: Arnold Hienemann, 1979, pp. 44-54.

Binns, Ronald. "The Novelist as Historian". <u>Critical Quarterly</u> Vol. 21, No. 2, pp. 70-72.

Blotner, Joseph L. <u>The Political Novel</u>. New York: Doubleday & Co. Inc., 1955.

(Blotner discusses the importance of the political novel in terms of the genre's interpretation of human experience. He also discusses the problems of definition of the political novel.)

Booth, Wayne C. <u>The Rhetoric of Fiction.</u> Chicago:-Chicago University Press, 1961.

Bradbury, Malcolm. Ed. <u>The Novel Today: Contemporary Writers on Modern Fiction</u>. Glasgow: Fontana,Collins, 1977.

Brander, Matthews. "The Historical Novel". <u>The Forum</u>, September 1897, pp. 79-91.

Burgess, Anthony. The Novel Now; A Student's Guide to Contemporary Fiction. London: Faber & Faber, 1967.

Butterfield, Herbert. The Historical Novel: An Essay. Cambridge: Cambridge University Press, 1924.

Fleishman, Avrom. The English Historical Novel: Walter Scott to Virginia Woolf. Baltimore & London: Johns Hopkins Press, 1971.

Ford, Paul Leicester. "The American Historical Novel". The Atlantic Monthly, December 1897, pp. 721-26.

Gay, Robert M. "The Historical Novel: Walter Edmunds". The Atlantic Monthly, May 1940, pp. 656-58.

Gerhardstein, Virginia Brokaw. Dickinson's American Historical Fiction. 4th Edn. Methuen & London: The Scarecrow Press, Inc., 1981.

Govindji. Hindilke Aitihasik Upanyasonmein Itihas Prayoq. Meexrut: Kalpana Prakashan, 1974.

Green, Peter. "Aspects of the Historical Novel". Essays By Divers Hands: Being the Transactions of the Royal society of literature, New Series, Vol. XXXI.,,,, London: OUP, 1972, pp. 35-60.

Halperin, John. Ed. The Theory of the Novel: New Essays. New York: OUP, 1974.

(The book deals with some of the more radical issues of contemporary novel-theory that have emerged along with the steady growth of interest in this century in the novel as a form.)

Henderson, Harry B. Versions of the Past: The Historical Imagination in American Fiction. New York: OUP, 197 4.

(Henderson hopes to create an appreciation of the self-awareness and complexity of the historical imagination of American writers. He does not propose a prescriptive, universal definition of the form of the historical novel.)

Hersey, John. "The Novel of Contemporary History". The Atlantic Monthly, November 1949, pp. 30-84.

Hervey, Allen. "History and the Novel". The Atlantic Monthly, February 1944, pp. 11.9-21.

Kantor, MacKinlay. "The Historical Novel". Three Views of the Novel: Lectures presented Under the Auspices of the Gertrude Clark whittal Poetry and Literature Fund. Washington: The Library Congress, 1957.

(Kantor lays stress on the accuracy of facts in a historical novel and believes that a historical novelist must be the historical expert knowing everything about the time he has chosen.)

Kermodey Frank. "Novels: History, and Type" Novel,- Vol.1. No. 3, 1968, pp. 231-38.

Lancaster, Bruce. "Inside of a Novel". The Atlantic Monthly, February 1946, pp. 75-78.

Lascelles, Mary. The Story-Teller Retrieves the Past: Historical Fiction and Fictitious History in the Art of Scott, Stevenson, Kipling and Some Others. Oxford: Clarenden Press, 1980.

Leisy, Ernest E. The American Historical Novel. Norman: University of Oklahoma Press, 1950.

(Leisy considers the historical novel as a very powerful cultural instrument in the new world and believes that the value of the historical novel, like that of any other form of fiction, rests on a valid hypothesis of human nature, regardless of locale.)

Levin, David. In Defense of Historical Literature: Essays on American History, Autobiography, Drama and Fiction. New York: Hill & Wang, 1967.

(Levin proposes to illustrate some of the advantages of examining history and biography with the eye of a literary critic; fiction and drama, with an interest in historical theory and fact.)

Lively, Robert. Fiction Fights the Civil War: An Unfinished Chapter in the Literary History of the American People Chapell Hill: The University of North Carolina Press, 1957,

(Lively does not believe in the widespread contempt for the historical novel that the critics persist in regarding the genre as 'a kind of mulelike animal begotten by the ass of fiction on the brood mare of fact, and hence, a sterile monster[1].)

Lukacs, Georg. <u>The Historical Novel</u>. Trans, by Hannah and Stanley. Harmondsworth: Penguin, 1969.

(Lukacs, from a Marxist point of view, points out that the historical novel is an extension of the novel of manners of the 18th century. The book provides a highly intellectual analysis of the novels of Scott, Cooper, Manzeni, Chekhov, and others.)

Malik, Yogendra K. Ed. <u>Politics and the Novel in India</u>. New Delhi: Orient Longman, 1978.

Marston, Doris Ricker. <u>A Guide to Writing History</u>. Cincinnati OH 45242: Writer Digest Division, F & W Publishing Corporation, 1976.

(Marston discusses the importance of viewpoint in writing the historical novel and provides certain rules in connection with the writing of the historical novel, the fact that makes his study prescriptive.)

Marriott, Sir John. <u>English History in English Fiction</u>. London: Blackie and Son, 1940.

Mazurek, Raymond A. "Metafiction, the Historical Novel, and Coover's 'The Public Burning"[1]. <u>Critique</u>, Vol. Xiu, No. 3, Spring 1982, pp. 29-41.

Morris, Wesley. <u>Toward a New Historicism</u>. Princeton:, Princeton University Press, 1972.

(Morris believes in the dual mode of existence of the literary work which necessitates a dual conception of literary meaning, that is, a work actually has two meanings: one determined by its historical context and a second, and less precise, meaning that derives from the critic's sense of the function of the work in his own, present, social context.)

Nield, Jonathan. <u>A Guide to the Best Historical Novels and Tales</u>. New York: Burt Franklin, 1968.

Pearce, Roy Harvey. <u>Historicism Once More; Problems and Occasions for the American Scholar</u>. Princeton: Princeton University Press, 1969.

(Writing from an Americanist's point of view, Pearce believes that we must study literary texts intrinsically as has been taught us by the New Criticism.)

Prescott, Orville. In My Opinion: An Inquiry into the Contemporary Novel. New York: Charter Books, 1952.

The Undying Past. New York: Doubleday & Co. Inc., 1961. (Writing about the historical novel, Prescott lays stress on certain basic attributes of human nature which are timeless; and believes that the historical novelist must not only make his characters human and interesting; he must make them creatures of their own times.)

Reed, Walter L. "Novel and History". An Exemplary History of the Novel; The Quixotic Versus the Picareque. Chicago: Chicago University Press, 1981, pp. 262-80.

Russel, B. Nye. "History and Literature: Branches of the Same Tree". Essays on History and Literature. Ed. R.H. Bremner. Columbus: Ohio State University Press, 1966.

Sanders, Andrew. The Victorian Historical Novel, 1840-1880. London: Macmillan, 1978.

Scott, Sir Walter. Ivanhoe. New York: Houghton Mifflin Co., 1923.

(In the 'Preface' Scott gives the distinction between Romance and a Novel.)

Sheppard, a.T. "The Historical Novel". London Quarterly Review October 193 2, pp. 245-58.

Simmons, James C. The Novelist As Historian. Paris: Mouton, 1973.

(The author throws light on Walter Scott as a historical novelist and discusses the historical element in the novels of Scott's contemporaries and followers.)

Speare, Morris E. The Political Novel: Its Development in England and America. New York: Russel & Russel, 1966.

(Speare discusses the political novel as a branch of the historical novel and provides a succinct description of the genre and points out the distinction between the two.)

Tourtellot, Arthur B. "History and the Historical Novel". The Saturday Review, August 24, 1940, pp. 3-4.

Trevelyan, G.M. "History and Fiction"* <u>Clio, a Kase and other Essays</u>. London: Longmans, Green & Co., T934, pp. 88-103.

Turner, Joseph W. "The Kinds qf Historical Fiction: An Essay in Definition and Methodology". <u>Genre</u>, Vol. 12, No. 3, 1979, pp. 333-55.

Waswo, F.ichard. "Story as Historiography in the 'Waverly Novels'". <u>English Literary History</u>, Vol. 47, 1980, pp. 304-30.

Weinstein, Mark A. "The Creative Imagination in Fiction and History". <u>Genre</u>, Vol. 9, No. 3, 1976, pp. 263-77.

White, Hayden. "The Fictions of Factual Representation". Ed. Angus Fletcher. <u>The Literature of Fact</u>. New York: Columbia University Press, 1976, pp. 21-44.

Wilding, Michael. <u>Political Fictions</u>. London: Routledge & Kegan Paul, 1980.

Williams, John. "Fact in Fiction: Problems for the Historical Novelist". <u>Denver Quarterly</u>, Vol. 7, No. 4, Winter 1973, pp. 1-12.

Other Works:

Abbas, K.A. <u>Tomorrow is Ours.</u> Bombay: Popular Book Depot, 1943

Allen, Charles. <u>Raj: A Scrapbook of British India, 1877-1947</u>. Harmondsworth: Penguin, 1979.

(Allen discusses various aspects of the British Raj, for instance,' the social order of the Raj, the position of Englishwomen in India, the off-duty pursuits of the Raj and the decline of British India.) ....

_____ - Ed. <u>Plain Tales from the</u> Raj; Images oJL.Bjriti.sh India <u>in the Twentieth</u> Century. London: Macdonald Futura Publishers, 1980.

Amirthnayagam, Guy. Ed. <u>Writers in East-West Encounter; New *Cv*" tural Bearings.</u> London: Macmillan, 1982.

Amur, G.S., Desai, S.K. Ed. <u>Colonial Consciousness in Commonwealth Literature</u>. Bombay: Somaiya Publications, 1984,

(Among the important themes discussed in these essays are: the regenerative role of colonialism in India, the Gandhian model for colonial epistemology, the dual consciousness of the commonwealth writers, etc.)

Anand, Mulk Raj. Untouchable. London: Wishart Books Ltd., 1935.

----- The Sword and the Sickle. London: Jonathan Cape, 1942.

----- Private Life of an Indian Prince. London: Bodley Head, 1970.

Bhattacharya, Bhabhani. So Many Hungers. Bombay: Hind Kitabs, 1947.

Brown, Hilton. Ed. The Sahibs. London: William Hodge, 1948.

Cameron, Roderick. "British Raj in India". Indo-British Review, Vols. 1 & 2, Nos. 4 & 1, April, September 1969, pp. 91-96.

Chamberlain, M.E. Britain and India; The Interaction of Two Peoples. Hamden; Archon Books, 1974.

Gollingwood, R.G. The Idea of History. London: OUP, rept. 1973.

(Collingwood considers how the modern idea of history has grown up from the time of Herodotus to the present day. To _____ history is not contained in books and documents, it lives only as a present interest and pursuit in the mind of the historian when he criticises and interprets those documents'.)

Curfcin, Philip D. "The Black Experience of Colonialism and Imperialism", Ed. Sidney Mintz. Slavery, Colonialism and Racism. New York: W.W. Norton & Co. Inc., 1974.

Dodwell, H.H. Ed. The Cambridge History of India: The Indian Empire. Vol. VI Delhi: S. Chand & Co. n.d.

Edwardes, Michael. British India, 1872-1947. London: Sidgwick and Jackson, 1967.

(The theme of this book is the meeting of civilizations and its consequences in the fields of human and state activity.)

_____ Raj: The Story of British India. London: Pan Books, 1967.

Fanon, Frantz. The Wretched of the Earth. Harmondsworth: Penguin, 1963.

(Fanon exposes the economic and psychological degradation of imperialism and points the way forward _ by violence if necessary - to socialism. This study of the Algerian revolution serves as a model for other liberation struggles.)

Ferrao, Nirmala. "We're a very Unsuccessful Nation". Interview with Charles Allen. Express Magazine, January 2, 1983, p. 6.

Forster, E.M. A Passage to India. London: Arnold, 1924.

--------The Hill of Devi, London; Arnold, 1953.

Gower, Herbert. A History of Indian-Literature. Delhi: Seema Publishers, 1975.

Green, Martin. Dreams of Adventure, Deeds of Empire. London & Henley: Routledge and Kegan Paul, 1980.

(Green studies the great tradition of adventure tales in English literature, from Defoe to Conrad and Kipling, linking them to the history of the British Empire and showing how they were the energizing myth of that empire. The book demonstrates that the" questioning imagination shaped by imperialism betrays buried obsessions with love and redemption, especially, in relation to the black people who feature prominently in all these tales.)

Greenberger, Allen J. "India: The Image as Reality". Indo-British Review, Vol. VI, No.s 3 & 4, pp. 65-68.

Griffiths, Sir Percival. The British Impact on India. London: Macdonald, 1952.

(The object of this book is to consider to what pattern the British Empire in India conformed, and in fact to answer the question as to whether the people of India have been affected for good or for ill by the British connection.)

Page NO. 323 not types

----- The Princess. New Delhi: Orient Longman, 1970.

Mannoni, 0. Prospero and Caliban: the Psychology of Colonization. London: Methuen & Co., 1950.

(The book is a classic study of the psychological aspect of the colonial problem with special reference to the study of Malagasy people in Madagaskar. Some of the conclusions of the book are of general applicability.)

Mason, Philip. A Shaft of Sunlight: Memories of a Varied Life. London: Andre Deutch, 1978.

Masters, John. Bugles and a Tiger: A Volume of Autobiography. New York: -1,956.

----- Bhowani Junction. London: Michael Joseph, 1954.

----- The Road Past Mandalay: A Personal Narrative. London: Michael Joseph, 1961.

Menezes, Naomi. "From the Raj to Rajiv". The Times of India Sunday Review, May 5, 1985, p. I.

Moraes, Frank, et al. Ed. India. Delhi: Vikas Publishing House, 1974.

(This book presents a portrait of India. It ranges far and wide across the subcontinent, covering history, politics and religion.)

Morris, John. Eating the Indian Air: Memories and Present Day Impressions. London: Hamish Hamilton, 1968.

Mosley, Leonard. The Last Days of the British Raj. , Bombay: Jaico, 1971.

Mukherjee, Meenakshi. The Twice Born Fiction, New Delhi: Hienemann Educational Books Ltd., 1971.

Mukherjee, Sujit. "Aspects of Indo-Anglian Novel". Quest, No. 65, April,June 1970, pp. 34-39.

Naik, M.K. et.al. Critical Essays on Indian Writing in English. Bombay: Macmillan, 1968.

----- Aspects of Indian Writing in English. Bortbay: Macmillan, 1980.

Nanporia, N.J. "Into Forster's India Again". The Times of. India Sunday Review, April 15, 1984, p. __I.

Orwell, George. Burmese Days. London: Gollancz, 1.935.

----- "Shooting an Elephant" (1936) . Selected Essays. Harmondsworth: Penguin, 1957.

Rao, Raja. Kanthapura. London: Allen & Unwin, 1938.

Sahagal, Nayantara. This Time of Morning. London: Victor Gollancz, 1965.

Said, Edward W. Orientalism. London & Henley: Routledge & Kegan Paul, 1978.

(Said has written a brilliant, highly imaginative history of the ways in which the West has discovered, invented and sought to control the East. This book is a subtle and farreaching critique of the attitudes that the West has traditionally assumed toward 'the Orient'.)

Sarma, G.P. Nationalism in Indo-Anqlian Fiction, New Delhi: Sterling Publishers (P) Ltd., 1978.

Shahane, V.A. S.'M. Forster; A Reassessment. Delhi: Kitab Mahal, 1963.

------- Ed. Perspectives on E.M. Forster's 'a Passage to India': A Collection of Critical Essays. New York: Barnes & Noble, 1968.

----- "Indo-Anglian Fiction and the Question of Form". The Journal of Indian Writing in English, July 1974.

Shirwadkar, Meena. Image of Woman in Indo-Anglian No; 3l. New Delhi: Sterling Publishing House Pvt. Ltd., 1979.

Simmel, George The Problems of the Philosophy of History: An Epistemological Essay. Translated and edited, with an introduction, by Guy Oakes. New York: The Free Press, 1977.

(The basic task of the book is the refutation of historical realism. Simmel discusses the concept of historical interpretation, the relationship between history, art, science and philosophy.)

Singh, Khushwant. Train to Pakistan. Bombay: Pearl Publications, 1957.

Singh, K. Natwar. E.M. Forster: A Tribute. New York: Harcourt Brace, 1964.

Singh, S.D. Novels on the Indian Mutiny. New Delhi: Arnold Hienemann, 1973.

Spear, Percival and Margaret. India Remembered. New Delhi: Orient Longman, 1981.

Trevelyan, Humphrey. The India We Left. London: Macmillan, 1972.

(The author believes that the Indian struggle for Independence was of not great historical significance and points out how the serious-minded Englishmen serving in India were concerned to find a moral justification for their presence as conquerors.)

Venkatramani, K.S. <u>Kandan, the Patriot</u>. Madras: Svetaranya Ashrama, 1932.

Williams, H.M. <u>Indp-Anglian Literature</u>. Bombay: Orient Longman, 1976.

Younghusband, F.E. <u>The Heart of a Continent</u>. London: 1896. London: 1896.

Reviews of Scott's novels:

<u>The Alien Sky</u> : (1953) :

Anon. <u>Bulletin from Virginia Kirkus ' Books_hpp_J3ervice</u>, July 15, 1953, p. 450.

Anon. <u>New York Herald Tribune Book Review,</u> October 13, 1953, p. 14.

Anon. <u>Times Literary Supplement</u>, September 25, 1953, p. 609.

May, Derwent. <u>New Statesman</u>, October 17, 1953, p. 462.

Metcalf, John. <u>Spectator</u>, September 25, 1953, p. 338.

Tweedy, M.J. <u>New York Times</u>, September 20, 1953, p. 26.

Wood, Percy. <u>Chicago Sunday Tribune</u>, October 25, 1953, p. 4.

<u>The Birds of Paradise</u> (1962) :

Anon. <u>Bulletin from Virginia Kirkus' Bookshop Service,</u> July 1, 1962, p. 588.

Anon. The Booklist, October 15, 1962, p. 165.

Anon. <u>Times Literary Supplement</u>, April 13, 1962, p. 245.

Ascherson, Neal, <u>New Statesman</u>, April 13, 1962, p. 533.

Cruttwell, Patrick. <u>Guardian</u>, April 13, 1962, p. 9.

Levin, Martin. <u>New York Times Book Review</u>, September 30, 1962, p. 44.

Mann, C.W, <u>Library Journal</u>, August 1962, p. 2778.

Manning, Olivia. <u>Spectator</u>, April 27, 1962, p. 559.

Schiller, Barbara. <u>New York Herotid Tribune Books</u>, October 28, 1962, p. 12.

Wood, Percy. <u>Chicago Sunday Tribune</u>, September 30, 1962, p. 12,

The Jewel in the Crown (1966) :

Anon. Times Literary Supplement, July 21, 1966, p. 629.

Bliven, Naomi. New Yorker, July 2, 1966, p. 66.

Dooley, E.A. Best Sellers, June 15, 1966, p. 122.

Levin, Martin. New York Times Book Review, July 17, 1966, p. 28.

Mann, C.W. Library Journal, October 1, 1966, p. 4703.

Mayne, Richard. New Statesman, July 22, 1966, p. 136.

The Day of. the Scorpion (1968) :

Anon. Times Literary Supplement, September 12, 1968, p. 975.

Duhamel, P.A. New York Times Book Review, November 10, 1968, p. 60.

Hopkinson, S.L. Library Journal, October 15, 1968, p. 3800.

Tindall, Gillian. New Statesman, September 6, 1968, p. 292.

The Towers of Silence (1971) :

Anderson, J.M. Best Sellers, March 15, 1972, p. 564.

Anon. Choice, July,August 197 2, p. 647.

Anon. Times Literary Supplement, October 8, 1971, p. 1199.

Davies, R.R. New Statesman, November 19, 1971, p. 706.

Foote, A.C. Book World, February 20, 1972, p. 6.

Hopkinson, S.L. Library Journal, February 15, 1972, p. 700.

Levin, Martin. New York Times Book Review, February 20, 1972, p. 26.

Ross, N.W. Saturday Review, June 24, 1972, p. 58.

Skow, John. "Eve of Empire". Time, March 27, 1972, p. 94.

A Division of the Spoils (197 5)

Andrews, C.R. Library Journal, September 15, 1975, p. 1654.

Anon. Times Literary Supplement, May 23, 1975, p. 555.

Cameron, James . New Stateaman, May 9, 1975,. p, 632.

Nye, Robert. Christian Science Monitor, October 10, 1975, p. 27.

Schott, Webster, New York Times Book Review, October 12, 1975, p. 34.

Sternman, William. Best Sellers, September 1975, p. 152.

Staying On (1977) :
Altbach, Philip G. Indian Book Chronicle, November 1, 1978, p. 365

Couto, Maria. "Memories and Legacies", Sunday Standard Magazine, January 18, 1981, p. 2.

Gardner, Marilyn. Christian Science Monitor, September 30, 1977, p. 26.

Gray, Paul. Time, July 18, 1977, p. 89.

Kilvert, Ian Scott. British Book News, May 15, 1977.

Leonard, John. "Love and Death in India". The New York Times, July 26, 1977.

Muggeridge, Malcolm. New York Times Book Review, August 21, 1977, p. 1.

Schuey, A..L. Library Journal, September 15, 1977, p. 1668.

Sivaratrik rishna, M. "Nostalgia for a Lost Empire". The Times of India Sunday Magazine, December 31, 1978.

Towers, Robert. Newsweek, August 8, 1977, p. 76.

Trachtenberg, Frances. Best Sellers, September 1977, p. 171.

Treglown, Jeremy. New Statesman, March 18, 1977, p. 366.

Wilkinson, Theon. Times Literary Supplement, March 18, 1977, p. 291.